sherri.yearg

250-8282

288-0803

Microsoft® Office
Outlook® 2003

Level 1

zooaltanta.org

Click 2X Panda Cam

Click in Picture if they have Border

Jeannine P. Pray

Microsoft® Office Outlook® 2003: Level 1

Part Number: 084680
Course Edition: 1.1

ACKNOWLEDGMENTS

Project Team

Content Developer: Jeannine P. Pray • **Content Manager:** Cheryl Russo • **Content Editors:** J-P Altieri and Laura Thomas • **Material Editor:** Elizabeth M. Fuller • **Graphic/Print Designers:** Benjamin Northern and Isolina Salgado • **Project Technical Support:** Michael Toscano

NOTICES

HELP US IMPROVE OUR COURSEWARE

Your comments are important to us. Please contact us at Element K Press LLC, 1-800-478-7788, 500 Canal View Boulevard, Rochester, NY 14623, Attention: Product Planning, or through our Web site at **http://support.elementkcourseware.com**.

NOTES

MICROSOFT® OFFICE OUTLOOK® 2003: LEVEL 1

LESSON 1: GETTING STARTED WITH OUTLOOK

A. Log On to Outlook 2

    Outlook 2

B. The Outlook Environment 5

    Microsoft Office Outlook 2003 Window 5

    Item 6

    Folder 7

C. Compose and Send a Simple Message 10

    Email 10

    The Message Form 11

    Email Addresses 12

D. Open a Message 16

    Message Symbols 16

E. Reply to a Message 18

    Reply Options 18

    The InfoBar 18

F. Print a Message 20

G. Delete a Message 22

LESSON 2: COMPOSING MESSAGES

A. Address a Message 26

    Address Book 26

    Global Address List 27

B. Format a Message 29

C. Check Spelling and Grammar 30

    AutoCorrect 30

Contents

D. Attach a File **33**

    Attachment 33

E. Forward a Message **35**

Lesson 3: Managing Mail

A. Open and Save an Attachment. **40**

B. Flag a Message **42**

C. Create a Folder **44**

D. Move Messages to a Folder **46**

E. Copy Messages to Folders **47**

F. Delete a Folder **49**

Lesson 4: Scheduling Appointments

A. The Outlook Calendar. **52**

    Calendar Entries. 52

    Views 52

B. Schedule an Appointment **55**

    The Appointment Form 55

    Calendar Symbols 56

C. Assign a Category to an Appointment **64**

    Category 64

D. Update Calendar Entries. **68**

Lesson 5: Scheduling Meetings

A. Schedule a Meeting **72**

    The Meeting Scheduling Process 72

    The Meeting Form 73

    Meeting Resources 74

Microsoft® Office Outlook® 2003: Level 1

B. Reply to a Meeting Request 78

C. Propose a New Meeting Time 81

D. Track Meeting Responses. 83

E. Update a Meeting Request 84

F. Cancel a Meeting Request 86

G. Print the Calendar 87

LESSON 6: MANAGING CONTACTS

A. Add a Contact 92

    Contacts 92

    The Contact Form 93

    The Outlook Address Book 93

B. Sort Contacts 97

    Sort Order 97

C. Find a Contact 100

D. Generate a Map 101

E. Edit a Contact 103

F. Delete a Contact 104

G. Print Contacts 105

LESSON 7: MANAGING TASKS

A. Create a Task 110

    Task 110

    The Task Form 111

Contents

B. Edit a Task 114

C. Update a Task 115

Lesson 8: Using Notes

A. Create a Note 118

B. Edit a Note... 121

C. Copy a Note.. 123

Appendix A: Microsoft Office Specialist Program

Lesson Labs 131

Solutions 137

Glossary 145

Index 147

Microsoft® Office Outlook® 2003: Level 1

ABOUT THIS COURSE

This course is the first in a series of three Microsoft® Office Outlook® courses. It will provide you with the skills you need to start sending and responding to email in Microsoft® Outlook® 2003, as well as maintaining your Calendar, scheduling meetings, and working with tasks and notes.

You are very busy these days. You can't keep up with all the correspondence, appointments, meetings, and tasks you need to accomplish. Therefore, it is essential to have a tool capable of keeping large amounts of information organized and at your fingertips. That tool is Outlook, and you can use it to effectively communicate electronically.

Course Description

Target Student

This course is designed for people with a basic understanding of Microsoft Windows who need to learn how to use Microsoft® Outlook® 2003 to compose and send email, schedule appointments and meetings, manage contact information and tasks, and use notes. This course is intended for persons interested in pursuing the Microsoft® Office Specialist certification for Outlook.

Course Prerequisites

This course assumes that you are familiar with using personal computers and have used a mouse and keyboard; basic typing skills are recommended. You should be comfortable in the Windows environment and be able to use Windows to manage information on your computer. Specifically, you should be able to: launch and close programs; navigate to information stored on the computer; and manage files and folders. The following courses are recommended, or you should have equivalent knowledge of:

- *Windows XP Professional: Level 1*
- *Windows XP Professional: Level 2*
- *Windows XP: Introduction*
- *Windows 2000: Introduction*

How to Use This Book

As a Learning Guide

Each lesson covers one broad topic or set of related topics. Lessons are arranged in order of increasing proficiency with *Microsoft® Outlook® 2003*; skills you acquire in one lesson are used and developed in subsequent lessons. For this reason, you should work through the lessons in sequence.

We organized each lesson into results-oriented topics. Topics include all the relevant and supporting information you need to master *Microsoft® Outlook® 2003*, and activities allow you to apply this information to practical hands-on examples.

You get to try out each new skill on a specially prepared sample file. This saves you typing time and allows you to concentrate on the skill at hand. Through the use of sample files, hands-on activities, illustrations that give you feedback at crucial steps, and supporting background information, this book provides you with the foundation and structure to learn *Microsoft® Outlook® 2003* quickly and easily.

As a Review Tool

Any method of instruction is only as effective as the time and effort you are willing to invest in it. In addition, some of the information that you learn in class may not be important to you immediately, but it may become important later on. For this reason, we encourage you to spend some time reviewing the topics and activities after the course. For additional challenge when reviewing activities, try the What You Do column before looking at the How You Do It column.

As a Reference

The organization and layout of the book make it easy to use as a learning tool and as an after-class reference. You can use this book as a first source for definitions of terms, background information on given topics, and summaries of procedures.

Microsoft® Outlook® 2003: Level 1 is one of a series of Element K courseware titles that addresses Microsoft® Office Specialist skill sets. The Office Specialist program is for individuals who use Microsoft's business desktop software and who seek recognition for their expertise with specific Microsoft products. Certification candidates must pass one or more product proficiency exams in order to earn Office Specialist certification.

Course Objectives

In this course, you will compose and send email, schedule appointments and meetings, manage contact information and tasks, and use notes.

You will:

- identify the components of the Outlook environment and compose and respond to a simple message.
- compose messages.
- use folders to manage mail.

- schedule appointments.
- schedule meetings.
- manage contacts and contact information.
- create and edit tasks.
- create and edit notes.

Course Requirements

Hardware

Active Directory Domain Controller and Exchange 2003 Server

For this course, you will need one computer for the classroom to run Windows Server 2003 Standard Edition and Exchange Server 2003 that meets the following system requirements:

- Pentium III 133 MHz (550 MHz recommended)
- 256 MB RAM (512 MB recommended)
- 10 GB disk space plus 700 MB for Exchange Server 2003
- CD-ROM or DVD drive
- VGA or higher video adapter and monitor
- Keyboard and Microsoft mouse or other input device

Classroom Computers

For this course, you will need one computer for each student and one for the instructor. Each computer will need the following minimum hardware components:

- A 233 MHz Pentium-class processor if you use Windows XP Professional as your operating system. 300 MHz is recommended.
- A 133 MHz Pentium-class processor if you use Windows 2000 Professional as your operating system.
- 128 MB of RAM.
- A 5 GB hard disk or larger if you use Windows XP Professional as your operating system. You should have at least 600 MB free hard-disk space available for the Office installation.
- A 3 GB hard disk or larger if you use Windows 2000 Professional as your operating system. You should have at least 600 MB free hard-disk space available for the Office installation.
- A floppy disk drive.
- A CD-ROM drive.
- A mouse or other pointing device.
- An 800 x 600 resolution monitor.
- Network cards and cabling for local network access.
- Internet access (see your local network administrator).

- A printer (optional).
- A projection system to display the instructor's computer screen.

Software

- Microsoft Windows Server 2003, Enterprise Edition.
- Microsoft Exchange Server 2003.
- Either Windows XP Professional with Service Pack 1a or later or Windows 2000 Professional with Service Pack 4 or later.
- Microsoft® Office Professional Edition 2003.

Class Setup

Active Directory Domain Controller and Exchange Server

If you already have an Active Directory domain controller, a DHCP server, DNS server, or mail server in your environment, you can use any or all of those server resources instead of creating a new server for class.

1. Complete an installation of Windows 2003 Server, Enterprise Edition on a blank hard drive.

    a. Press Enter at the Welcome Setup screen.

    b. Accept the license agreement.

    c. Create an 8 GB NTFS partition.

    d. If necessary, modify the default Setup Options (installation location, accessibility options, language) as appropriate for your learning environment.

    e. If necessary, modify the default Regional and Language Options as appropriate for your learning environment.

    f. Enter your name and organization.

    g. Enter the product key.

    h. Enter the appropriate number of Per Server licenses for your learning environment.

    i. Enter an appropriate computer name and a password for the Administrator account. (This training was developed using a computer name of *Titanium*, and an Administrator password of *Passw0rd*, with a capital "P" and where "0" is a zero.)

    j. Select the Date And Time and Time Zone settings appropriate for your learning environment.

    k. Select Custom Networking Settings and assign the computer a manual IP address appropriate for your learning environment (see your network administrator for a valid IP address). For example, we have listed the following Custom Network Settings:

    — Enter IP #: 192.168.100.200

    — Enter Sub Net Mask: 255.255.255.0

    — Enter DNS #: 192.168.100.200

    — Enter Default Gateway #: See your network administrator.

    l.   Configure the computer to be a member of the workgroup named *WORKGROUP*. (You will make this computer an Active Directory domain controller for its own domain later.)

2.   Press Ctrl+Alt+Delete and log on as the Administrator.

3.   At the Manage Your Server window, check the Don't Display This Page At Logon check box and close the window.

4.   To install the computer as an Active Directory domain controller, run the Configure Your Server Wizard.

    a.   From the taskbar, choose Start→Run.

    b.   In the Open text box, type *dcpromo* and click OK.

    c.   In the Active Directory Installation Wizard dialog box, click Next.

    d.   In the Operating System Compatibility dialog box, click Next.

    e.   Verify that Domain Controller For A New Domain is selected and click Next.

    f.   Verify that Domain In A New Forest is selected and click Next.

    g.   In the Full DNS Name For New Domain dialog box, type *xchg.com* and click Next.

    h.   Accept the default Domain NetBIOS name *xchg* and click Next.

    i.   Accept the default Database Folder and Log Folder and click Next.

    j.   Accept the default folder location for the Shared System Volume and click Next.

    k.   Verify that the Install And Configure The DNS Server On This Computer, And Set This Computer To Use The DNS Server As Its Preferred DNS Server option is selected and click Next.

    l.   Verify that Permissions Compatible Only With Windows 2000 Or Windows Server 2003 Operating Systems is selected and click Next.

    m.   Type an appropriate Restore Mode Password and confirm. (This course was developed with a Restore Mode password of *Passw0rd*.) Click Next.

    n.   In the Summary dialog box, click Next.

    o.   To close the Active Directory Installation dialog box, click Finish.

    p.   When prompted, click Restart Now.

5.   Press Ctrl+Alt+Delete and log on as the Administrator.

6.   Add and remove necessary Windows Components.

    a.   From the taskbar, choose Start→Control Panel→Add Or Remove Programs.

    b.   Click Add/Remove Windows Components.

    c.   Uncheck the Internet Explorer Enhanced Security Configuration check box.

    d.   Click the words "Application Server" and click Details.

    e.   In the Application Server dialog box, check the ASP.NET check box.

    f.   Click the words "Internet Information Services (IIS)" and click Details.

    g.   In the Internet Information Services (IIS) dialog box, check the NNTP Service and the SMTP Service check boxes and click OK twice.

    h.   Click Next to begin Setup.

    i.   If necessary, insert CD-ROM to begin Setup.

    j.   To close the Windows Components Wizard, click Finish.

    k.   Close the Add Or Remove Programs window.

l.   Restart the computer.

7.   Press Ctrl+Alt+Delete and log on as the Administrator.

8.   Install Windows Support Tools.

    a.   If necessary, insert the Windows Server 2003 CD-ROM.

    b.   When it automatically starts, click Exit.

    c.   Use Windows Explorer to browse to the Support\Tools folder on the CD-ROM.

    d.   Double-click Suptools.msi

    e.   At the Windows Support Tools Setup Wizard window, click Next.

    f.   Agree to the End-User License Agreement and click Next.

    g.   At the User Information screen, click Next.

    h.   Accept the default destination directory of C:\Program Files\Support Tools and click Install Now.

    i.   Click Finish.

    j.   Eject the Windows Server 2003 CD-ROM.

9.   Run Dcdiag.exe and Netdiag.exe.

    a.   In Windows Explorer, navigate to C:\Program Files\Support Tools.

    b.   Double-click Dcdiag.exe to run it.

    c.   Double-click Netdiag.exe to run it.

    d.   Close Windows Explorer.

10.   Install Microsoft Exchange Server 2003.

    a.   Insert the Microsoft Exchange Server 2003 CD-ROM.

    b.   In the Microsoft Exchange Server 2003 window, click Exchange Deployment Tools.

    c.   Click Deploy The First Exchange 2003 Server.

    d.   Click New Exchange 2003 Server.

    e.   In the New Exchange 2003 Installation checklist, check steps 1, 2, 3, 4, and 5.

    f.   In step 6 on the checklist, click Run ForestPrep Now.

        —   In the Microsoft Exchange Installation Wizard window, click Next.

        —   Agree to the License Agreement and click Next.

        —   Accept the default Component Selection and click Next.

        —   Accept the default Microsoft Exchange Server Administrator Account and click Next.

        —   Click Finish.

        —   Check the step 6 check box.

    g.   In step 7, click Run DomainPrep Now.

        —   In the Microsoft Exchange Installation Wizard window, click Next.

        —   Agree to the License Agreement and click Next.

        —   Accept the default Component Selection and click Next.

        —   If prompted, in the Microsoft Exchange Installation warning, click OK.

        —   Click Finish.

        —   Check the step 7 check box.

    h.   In step 8, click Run Setup Now.

— In the Microsoft Exchange Installation Wizard window, click Next.

— Agree to the License Agreement and click Next.

— Accept the default Component Selection and click Next.

— Accept the default Installation Type of Create A New Exchange Organization and click Next.

— Enter an organization name. (This course was developed using the Exchange organization name of *WhiteMetal*.) Click Next.

— Agree to the Licensing Agreement and click Next.

— At the Installation Summary, click Next.

— Click Finish.

— Check the step 8 check box.

— Close the Exchange Server Deployment Tools window.

 i. Click Exit to close the Microsoft Exchange Server 2003 window.

11. Restart the computer and log on as the Administrator.

12. Disable password complexity requirements.

 a. From the taskbar, choose Start→Administrative Tools→Domain Security Policy.

 b. Under Security Settings, expand Account Policies.

 c. Click Password Policy.

 d. In the right pane, double-click Password Must Meet Complexity Requirements.

 e. Check the Define This Policy Setting check box.

 f. Verify that Disable is selected.

 g. Click OK.

 h. Double-click Minimum Password Length.

 i. Check the Define This Policy Setting check box.

 j. In the Password Must Be At Least spin box, type *8*.

 k. Click OK.

 l. Close the Default Domain Security Settings window.

13. Refresh the user policy.

 a. From the taskbar, choose Start→Run.

 b. Type *gpupdate* and click OK.

14. Create a domain user account for each student in the class. (This course was developed using a first name of *Student*, a last name of *##*, user logon names of *Student##* and a password of *password*. For instance, the instructor was *Student00*, the first student was *Student01*, and so on.)

 a. From the Start menu, choose Administrative Tools→Active Directory Users and Computers.

 b. Click the organization name to expand it.

 c. Right-click Users and choose New→User to create a new user.

 d. Enter First Name *Student*

 e. Enter Last Name *##*

 f. Enter user logon name *Student##* (with no spaces) and click Next.

 g. Enter a password of *password* and confirm it.

h.   Uncheck the User Must Change Password At Next Logon check box.

i.   Check the User Cannot Change Password and the Password Never Expires check boxes and click Next twice.

j.   Click Finish.

k.   Repeat steps c through j until all student domain user accounts have been created.

15. It is recommended that after you have all software installed, you connect to Microsoft's Windows Update site to download and install any updates.

16. Restart the computer and log on as the Administrator.

17. On the server, in the Exchange System Manager, create a new Address Book called Resources. Under All Global Address List, add/grant the Exchange Users group Full Control permissions. Close the window.

18. On the server, display the Active Directory. In the Users And Computers window, create a Global Distribution Group called Resources.

19. Create user accounts for each resource: Conference Room A, Conference Room B, and TV VCR.

20. In the Properties Of Resources window, click Modify. Click Find Now. Scroll to the Resources group and select it. Click OK. Then click OK again to close the Resources Properties sheet.

On Each Student WorkStation:

1. Install Windows 2000 Professional or Windows XP Professional on an empty partition.

    —   Leave the Administrator password blank.

    —   For all other installation parameters, use values that are appropriate for your environment (see your local network administrator if you need details).

2. On Windows 2000 Professional, when the Network Identification Wizard runs after installation, select the Users Must Enter A User Name And Password To Use This Computer option. (This step ensures that students will be able to log on as the Administrator user regardless of what other user accounts exist on the computer.)

3. On Windows 2000 Professional, in the Getting Started with Windows 2000 window, uncheck Show This Screen At Startup. Click Exit.

4. On Windows 2000 Professional, set 800 x 600 display resolution: right-click the desktop and choose Properties. Select the Settings tab. Move the Screen Area slider to 800 x 600 Pixels. Click OK twice, then click Yes.

5. On Windows 2000 Professional, install Service Pack 4. Use the Service Pack installation defaults.

6. On Windows XP Professional, disable the Welcome screen. (This step ensures that students will be able to log on as the Administrator user regardless of what other user accounts exist on the computer.) Choose Start and choose Control Panel→User Accounts. Click Change The Way Users Log On And Off. Uncheck Use Welcome Screen. Click Apply Options.

7. On Windows XP Professional, install Service Pack 1. Use the Service Pack installation defaults.

8. On either operating system, install a printer driver (a physical print device is optional).

    —   For Windows XP Professional, choose Start→Printers And Faxes. Under Printer Tasks, click Add A Printer and follow the prompts.

— For Windows 2000 Professional, choose Start→Settings→Printers. Run the Add Printer Wizard and follow the prompts.

9. Verify that file extensions are visible.

10. Run the Internet Connection Wizard to set up the Internet connection as appropriate for your environment, if you did not do so during installation.

11. Log on to the computer as the Administrator user if you have not already done so.

12. Perform a Complete installation of Microsoft® Office Professional Edition 2003.

13. Minimize the Language Bar if it appears.

14. Configure Microsoft® Outlook®:

— From the Taskbar, choose Start→Control Panel.

— In the Control Panel, click User Accounts.

— Click the Mail icon.

— In the Mail Setup dialog box, click Show Profiles.

— In the Mail dialog box, select Prompt For A Profile To Be Used.

— Click Add.

— In the New Profile dialog box, enter the profile name (for example, Student01) and click OK to launch the E-mail Accounts Wizard.

— In the E-mail Accounts Wizard, under the E-mail heading, select Add A New E-mail Account and click Next.

— Select Microsoft Exchange Server, and then click Next.

— Enter your server name and the user name for the workstation.

— Click the More Settings button.

— Enter the password and click OK.

— In the Microsoft Exchange Server dialog box, select the Connection tab. Select Connect Using My Local Area Network (LAN), and click OK. (Both the server and user name should now be underlined, which confirms account information. If they aren't, click Check Name to perform the verification.)

— Click Next.

— Click Finish.

— In the Mail dialog box, click OK.

— Close the User Accounts window.

— On the Windows desktop, choose Start→E-mail Microsoft Outlook.

— Select the appropriate profile for the student workstation, and then enter the password.

— If necessary, maximize the window.

For the Instructor:

1. Log on to each Student workstation as the Administrator user.

2. On each Student workstation, extract the course data files from the CD-ROM provided with the course manual. On the course CD-ROM, open the 084_680 folder. Then, open the Data folder. Run the 084680dd.exe self-extracting file located within. This will install a folder named 084680Data on your C drive. This folder contains all the data files that you will use to complete this course.

3. On each Student workstation, copy the Contacts from the 084680Data folder to the Contacts folder in Microsoft® Office Outlook® 2003. *Please see "Method 1 (or 2 or 3) of Installing the Contacts from the Course CD-ROM" below for more information regarding this process.*

4. From the Instructor workstation, send a meeting request from the Instructor to all users in the class and the resources, Conference Room A and TV VCR. The date of the meeting is one week from the upcoming Tuesday. The time is 2:00 P.M. to 4:00 P.M. The subject of the meeting is Vacation Policy.

5. From the Instructor workstation, send the two messages displayed in the following graphics to all users in the class.

Subject:	New Job Posting

Below is a brief description of the job posting for the Technical Writer position. Let me know what you think.

Responsibilities include developing courseware content, instructor materials, self-paced learning products, participating in classroom sessions as needed, and staying current with the computer industry.

Subject:	System Training

This is a reminder about the upcoming system training sessions. Make sure the members of your group attend one of the following:

- Monday, 1-3, Room C
- Wednesday, 10-11, Room A
- Thursday, 3-4, Seminar Room

On another note, below are the new rates for health insurance.

- Single - $38
- Single with Children - $66
- Family - $87

6. Provide place cards identifying each computer's user name (Student ##). The entire class should be able to see each card.

7. Before you begin, assign students to work in pairs.

Method 1 of Installing the Contacts from the Course CD-ROM

There are three main ways to install the contact available on the course CD-ROM into Microsoft® Office Outlook® 2003.

The first, most common method is:

1. As stated above, extract the data files from the course CD-ROM to the 084680Data folder on your C drive.

2. Open this folder in Windows Explorer.

3. Choose Start→All Programs→Microsoft Office→Microsoft Office Outlook 2003 to open Microsoft® Office Outlook® 2003.

4. Return to Windows Explorer and select all of the MSG files within the 084680Data folder.

5. Choose Edit→Copy.

6. Return to Microsoft® Office Outlook® 2003.

7. Open the Contacts view in Outlook.

8.   Choose Edit→Paste.

Method 2 of Installing the Contacts from the Course CD-ROM

Drag-and-Drop Technique:

1.   Open Windows Explorer and navigate to C:\084680Data, where the data files should have been extracted from the course CD-ROM.

2.   Select all of the MSG files by clicking the first MSG file with you mouse, hold down Shift and click the last MSG file.

3.   Choose Start→All Programs→Microsoft Office→Microsoft Office Outlook 2003 to open Microsoft® Office Outlook® 2003.

4.   Click the Contacts tab.

5.   Position both the Windows Explorer window and Outlook 2003 side-by-side on your screen.

6.   Drag-and-drop the contacts into the empty Contacts window in Outlook 2003.

7.   The contacts should appear in alphabetical order, starting with Bennett Anderson and ending with Jeff Rice.

Method 3 of Installing the Contacts from the Course CD-ROM

An alternate, more time consuming (but more reliable) technique is to perform the following:

1.   Choose Start→All Programs→Microsoft Office→Microsoft Office Outlook 2003 to open Microsoft® Office Outlook® 2003.

2.   Click the Contacts tab.

3.   Click the New Contact button.

4.   In the New Contact dialog box, choose Insert→File.

5.   Navigate to C:\084680Data, where the data files should have been extracted from the course CD-ROM.

6.   Select one of the MSG files and select Insert.

7.   The file will appear as an attachment within the current open New Contact dialog box.

8.   Double-click the attached MSG file to open it in its own New Contact dialog box.

9.   In the open New Contact dialog box, click Save And Close.

10. The MSG file is now added to the Contacts list as a new contact in Outlook 2003.

11. Repeat steps 4-10 until all of the contacts are added. When finished, close the empty New Contact dialog box and select No when prompted to save changes to the empty contact file.

List of Additional Files

Printed with each activity is a list of files students open to complete that activity. Many activities also require additional files that students do not open, but are needed to support the file(s) students are working with. These supporting files are included with the student data files on the course CD-ROM or data disk. Do not delete these files.

NOTES

Lesson 1

Getting Started with Outlook

Lesson Time
40 minutes to 50 minutes

Lesson Objectives:

In this lesson, you will identify the components of the Outlook environment and compose and respond to a simple message.

You will:

*   Log on to Outlook.

*   List the components of the Outlook environment.

*   Compose and send a simple message.

*   Open a message.

*   Reply to a message.

*   Print a message.

*   Delete a message.

Introduction

Many of us have to handle large amounts of business communications, including correspondence. Therefore, the logical place to start in Microsoft® Office Outlook® 2003 is with mail. In this lesson, you will create and respond to a mail message.

You are working your way through stacks of correspondence. Wouldn't it be great if there was a more effective way to correspond with others? By using Outlook, you can compose, send, and reply to messages quickly and easily, enabling you to efficiently and effectively handle your correspondence.

TOPIC A

Log On to Outlook

Before you can use Outlook, you need to log on so that Outlook recognizes you as an authorized user. In this topic, you will log on to Outlook.

Just as you might need to follow a process to access resources within an office building, you need to follow a log on process to access Outlook. Once you are logged on, you can begin communicating electronically with others.

Outlook

Definition:

Outlook is a software program that includes email, the Calendar, Contacts, the Tasks list, Notes, and the Journal that you can use to electronically communicate with others and manage personal information.

Example:

Figure 1-1 displays examples of how you can use Outlook to communicate electronically.

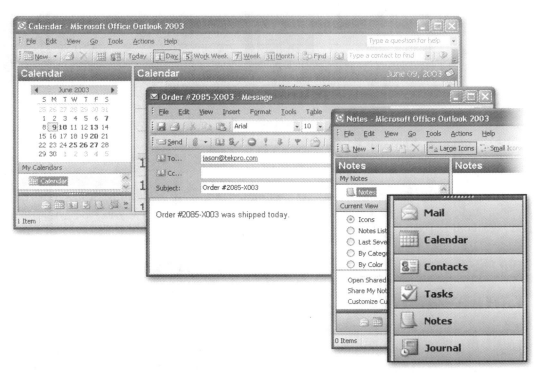

Figure 1-1: *Outlook tasks.*

How to Log On to Outlook

Procedure Reference: Log On to Outlook

To log on to Outlook:

1. On the Windows taskbar, click Start. The Start menu is displayed.

2. Choose All Programs→Microsoft Office→Microsoft Office Outlook 2003. The Connect To dialog box is displayed.

3. In the Password text box, enter your password.

4. Click OK. Outlook is opened.

5. In the upper-right corner of the window, click the Maximize button.

ACTIVITY 1-1

Logging On to Outlook

Setup:

The Windows XP desktop is displayed. No windows are open. Your instructor has given you your user name and password.

Scenario:

Your company uses Outlook to manage communication and scheduling. You've never used Outlook before. You have Outlook installed on your computer, and you have your user name and password, so you're ready to start.

What You Do	How You Do It
1. Launch Outlook.	a. On the Windows taskbar, **click Start to display the Start menu.**
	b. **Choose All Programs→Microsoft Office→ Microsoft Office Outlook 2003** to display the Connect To dialog box.
	This course was developed in Microsoft Windows XP Professional. How you start Outlook might differ slightly from this step if you are not using the same operating system.
	If the PC is set up for multiple users, you can use the Profile Name drop-down list box in the Choose Profile dialog box to select a user.
	c. In the Password text box, **enter your password**
	d. **Click OK** to open Outlook.
2. Maximize the Outlook window.	a. In the upper-right corner of the window, **click the Maximize button** ▣ .
3. What components of the Outlook window look familiar to you?	

TOPIC B

The Outlook Environment

Your first step when working with Outlook is to determine how it works. By understanding the basics of the software, you will have a solid foundation upon which to build toward more critical skills. In this topic, you will explore the Outlook application and identify window components.

When you need to use an item for the first time, it's important to become familiar with the item's components before you start using it. The same is true for Outlook. By knowing the components of Outlook, it will be easier to use and you will be able to work more efficiently because you are familiar with the environment.

Microsoft Office Outlook 2003 Window

After you log on, the Microsoft Office Outlook 2003 window is displayed. Its components are listed in the following table.

Component	What It Does
Title bar	Displays the name of the current folder and the application.
Menu bar	Lists the menus.
Ask A Question box	Provides a place to enter questions.
Standard toolbar	Provides quick access to some of the most frequently used commands.
Navigation Pane	The column on the left side of the window that provides access to all components of Outlook.
Task pane	Provides a window that you can use to access commonly used commands.
Go Menu	Part of the Navigation Pane that allows you to quickly switch between components.
Quick Launch bar	Part of the Navigation Pane that provides quick access to frequently used components.
Reading Pane	Displays the contents of the selected message without opening the message.
Status bar	Displays information about the active folder.

Figure 1-2 displays the components of the Microsoft Office Outlook 2003 window.

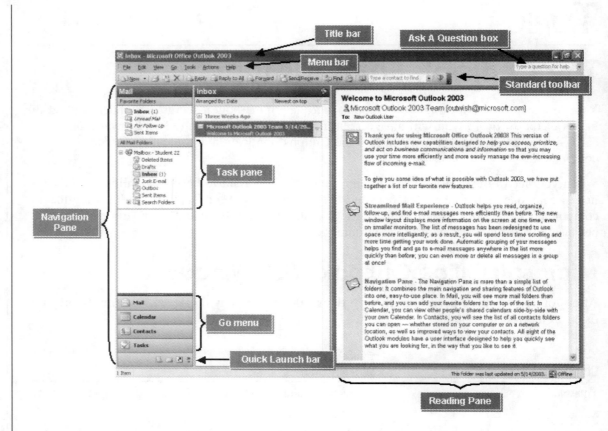

Figure 1-2: *The components of the Microsoft Office Outlook 2003 window.*

Item

Definition:

An *item* is a basic element created in Outlook that holds information and is stored in a specific location.

Example:

Figure 1-3 displays an example of an item in Outlook.

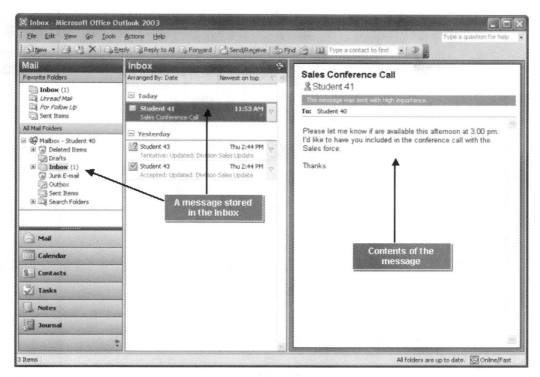

Figure 1-3: *A message item in Outlook.*

Outlook Items

Items in Outlook include:

- Messages
- Appointments
- Meetings
- Contacts
- Tasks
- Notes

Folder

Definition:

A *folder* is a tool that you can use to store and organize Outlook items.

Example:

Figure 1-4 displays an example of a folder in Outlook.

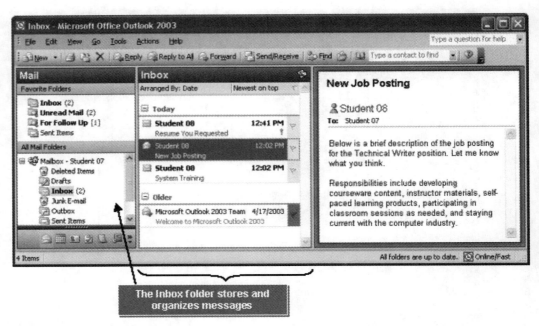

Figure 1-4: *A folder in Outlook.*

The Outlook Environment

Outlook contains six main components that you can use to communicate with others. These components are folders and are listed in the following table.

Component	Description
Inbox	Where you send and receive messages.
Calendar	Where you schedule appointments, meetings, and events.
Contacts	Where you enter and track business and personal contacts.
Tasks List	Where you create and manage tasks.
Notes	Where you quickly record reminders.
Journal	Where you can automatically track all items that you have specified as they occur.

Additional Outlook Folders

Additional folders in Outlook include:

- Deleted Items—Stores any items that you delete in Outlook.
- Drafts—Stores copies of unfinished messages you can complete and send at a later time.
- Junk E-mail—Contains junk email messages.
- Outbox—Temporarily stores messages you send until they are delivered.
- Sent Items—Stores copies of messages you send to others.
- Sync Issues—Contains all of the synchronization logs.

- Search Folders—Contain views of mail items that satisfy specific search criteria.

Help

While you're using Outlook, you can use the following resources if you need help:

- The Type A Question For Help box located on the Menu bar.
- Microsoft Outlook Help task pane, which you can display by choosing Help→ Microsoft Outlook Help.

ACTIVITY 1-2

Exploring the Outlook Environment

Setup:

The Outlook window is displayed.

Scenario:

Before you can begin using Outlook efficiently, it's a good idea to spend some time familiarizing yourself with the Outlook environment.

What You Do	How You Do It

1. **Match the components of the Outlook window with their corresponding definitions.**

Navigation Pane

Quick Launch bar

Go Menu

Reading Pane

Status bar

a. Displays the contents of the selected message without opening the message.

b. Displays information about the active folder.

c. The column on the left side of the Outlook window that provides access to all components of Outlook.

d. Part of the Navigation Pane that allows you to quickly switch between Mail, Calendar, Contacts, and Tasks.

e. Part of the Navigation Pane that provides quick access through buttons to frequently used Outlook components.

2. **Identify the buttons on the Standard toolbar.**

a. On the Standard toolbar, **point to the first button** [New ▾] . A ToolTip is displayed, indicating the name of the button. You can use this button to create a new mail message in Outlook.

b. Using ToolTips, **identify some of the other buttons on the Standard toolbar.**

3. Display the short and expanded versions of the File menu.

    a. On the menu bar, **choose File** to display the short menu.

    b. At the bottom of the short menu, **click the Expand arrow** to display the expanded menu.

    c. On the menu bar, **click File** to close the File menu.

TOPIC C

Compose and Send a Simple Message

You are familiar with Outlook and the environment, and you're ready to start communicating. In this topic, you will compose and send mail messages.

You need to send some important information to a client who is located in another part of the country. The client needs the information today. Sending it by regular mail is not an option. The client is out of the office, so you can't call him either. By using Outlook, you can quickly and efficiently send the information in a simple message.

Email

Electronic mail, or *email*, is an application that allows a user to create, send, and receive electronic messages. You can send information and receive information from users within your network of computers or outside your network of computers via the Internet.

Figure 1-5 displays an example of the flow of email.

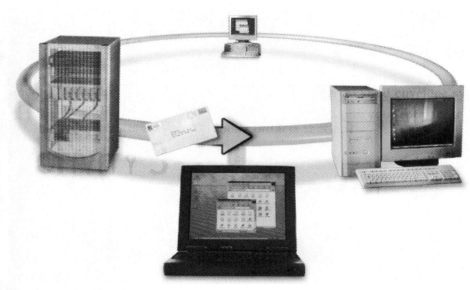

Figure 1-5: *The flow of email inside a network of computers and via the Internet.*

The Message Form

When you create a new message, Outlook displays a Message form that contains text boxes in which you can enter specific information. The four main text boxes in a Message form are listed in Table 1-1.

Table 1-1: *Message Form Text Boxes*

Text Box	Information to Enter
To	Email address or user name of the person to whom you want to send the message.
Cc	Email address or user name of anyone who you want to receive a copy of the message (Carbon Copy).
Subject	A brief description of the message.
Message Body	The text of the message.

Figure 1-6 displays an example of a completed Message form.

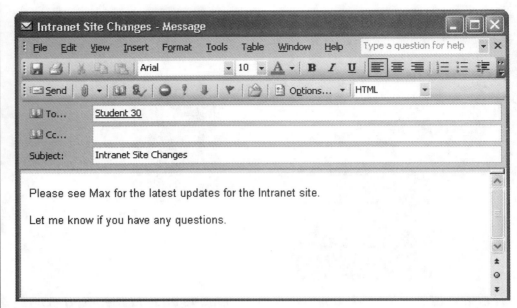

Figure 1-6: *A completed Message form.*

Default Mail Editor

Microsoft Word is the default mail editor for Outlook. Therefore, when you create mail messages, you will have access to a number of Word features, making it easier to create messages in Outlook.

Email Addresses

Definition:

An *email address* is a string used to specify the user name and location where users can send you email.

Example:

Figure 1-7 displays some examples of email addresses.

Figure 1-7: *Examples of email addresses.*

How to Compose and Send a Message

Procedure Reference: Compose and Send a Message

To compose and send a new message:

1.   On the Standard toolbar, click New. A new Message form is displayed.

2. In the To text box, type the name of the user to whom you want to address the message.

    📌 If you are addressing the message to more than one recipient, separate the user names with a semicolon (;).

    📌 In the To text box, an underlined user name indicates that it matches a name on the server.

    📌 Although most messages will contain a subject and some text in the message body, only the To text box must be filled in to send a message.

3. Click in the Subject field.

4. Enter a subject of your choice.

5. Press Tab to move to the message body text box.

6. Enter a message.

7. If desired, press Enter twice and type your name.

8. On the Standard toolbar, click Send to send the message.

    📌 When the message arrives at its destination, a message alert is displayed briefly in the lower-right corner of the Outlook window. It contains the sender's name, the subject, and the first few words of the message.

Email Etiquette

Net etiquette, or Network etiquette, is a set of guidelines for ethical behavior on the Internet, including sending and receiving email. You can become a responsible Internet citizen by applying the guidelines outlined in the following list.

- Think twice before clicking the Send button. Once you send an email message, you might not be able to take it back.

- Realize that an email message can be easily circulated (forwarded, printed and distributed, and so on).

- Be cautious with humor and sarcasm. Statements that are funny person-to-person might lose their humor in writing and appear, instead, confusing or even vicious.

- Use emoticons (emotion icons), or smileys, to convey subtle emotional tones that cannot be adequately expressed in written words. The following table displays a few of the emoticons (look at them sideways):

Emoticon	Conveys
:-)	Cheeriness
;-)	Light sarcasm (a wink)
:-(	Displeasure or sadness
:-()	Alarm
:~?	Confusion
:-D	Laughter

Emoticon	Conveys
:-l	Boredom or indifference
:-o	Surprise

- Use smileys sparingly; they can be tedious to read.

- Avoid typing in all uppercase letters when emphasizing words—it seems like shouting.

- Never send unsolicited advertisements to email recipients or newsgroups. This is called *spamming*, and it's a serious Internet offense.

- Keep the line length of your message or posting to 60 or fewer characters. Some users' screens cannot display more than 60 characters per line.

- Use descriptive subjects so that your messages are easier to find and file.

- Follow a newsgroup's discussions for a while to familiarize yourself with its objectives and general tone before you begin posting articles. This technique is called lurking; posting your first message is called delurking.

- Read the FAQs (Frequently Asked Questions) of a newsgroup before you start posting articles. Most groups have FAQs for new subscribers.

- Post your test articles to a test group, such as alt.test or misc.test. Posting tests to non-test newsgroups is considered rude.

- Take a moment to decide whether it's more appropriate to respond privately to an individual's post in a mailing list or newsgroup than to respond publicly to the whole list or group.

- Don't engage in rampant *flaming* (responding harshly or insultingly to an email or posting). Flame wars can be very ugly.

Net etiquette is a serious topic. If you post inappropriate material—unsolicited advertisements, inflammatory or insulting remarks, misinformation, and so on—to mailing lists or newsgroups, there is a good chance you'll be flamed publicly (in newsgroup postings) or privately (in email). In extreme cases, Net etiquette violators can be banished from a mailing list or newsgroup.

Save Messages

While composing a message, you might decide that you are not ready to send the message. You can save a message and send it at a later time by choosing File→Save. The message is stored in the Drafts folder. When you're ready to finish the message, simply open the message, add the desired information to the Message form, and send the message.

ACTIVITY 1-3

Composing and Sending a Simple Message

Setup:
The Outlook window is maximized. The contents of the Inbox are displayed. You have been assigned to work with another student.

Scenario:
You're employed at TekPro, an employment agency. You received a request for information from a prospective applicant asking how she can register with your agency. You need to have her send you her resume.

What You Do	How You Do It
1. **Create a new message. Address it to your partner with a subject of *Registration Information*.**	a. On the Standard toolbar, **click New** ![New]. A new Message form is displayed.
	b. In the To text box, **type your partner's user name.**
	c. **Click in the Subject field.**
	d. **Type *Registration Information***
2. **Enter the text of the message and send the message.**	a. **Press Tab** to move to the message body text box.
	b. **Type *Thank you for your interest in our agency. To register with us, please send us your resume.***
	c. **Press Enter twice.**
	d. **Type your name.**
	e. On the Standard toolbar, **click Send** ![Send].

TOPIC D

Open a Message

You know how to compose and send messages. But, what will you do when someone else sends you a message? In this topic, you will open a message.

Your Inbox contains an important message from a client for which you have been waiting. Unless you open the message, you won't know what the contents of the message include.

Message Symbols

Each message in your Inbox displays with one or more message symbols next to it. The symbols represent the type or status of the message.

Examples of Message Symbols

Table 1-2 displays message symbols.

Table 1-2: *Message Symbols*

Symbol	Description
❗	High importance message
⬇	Low importance message
✉	A read message
✉	An unread message
✉	A replied message
✉	A forwarded message
📎	Message has an attachment
🚩	Message is flagged for follow-up
✓	Message is flagged as complete

How to Open a Message

Procedure Reference: Open a Message

To open a message:

1. In the Inbox, open a message.
    *   Double-click the message you want to open.
    *   Select the message you want to open and choose File→Open→Selected Items.
    *   Right-click the message you want to open and choose Open.
    *   Select the message you want to open and press Enter.

    📌 You don't have to open a message to read it. You can read the contents of a message by using the Reading Pane.

ACTIVITY 1-4

Opening a Message

Data Files:

* New Job Posting.msg

Setup:

The contents of the Inbox are displayed.

Scenario:

One of your clients has an open position for a Technical Writer. You have some candidates in mind for the position, but you've been waiting for the job description from your co-worker to make sure the candidates are qualified. You just received a message from your co-worker. You hope the message contains the information for which you've been waiting.

What You Do	How You Do It

1. **How does a new, unread message display in the Inbox?**

   a) The header is bold.

   b) The header is red.

   c) The header contains a closed envelope symbol.

   d) The header contains an open envelope symbol.

   e) The header contains the sender's user name.

2. **Open the New Job Posting message.**   a. In the Inbox, **double-click the New Job Posting message** to open it.

TOPIC E

Reply to a Message

You have created, sent, and received email messages. What if you receive an email that requires you to reply? In this topic, you will open and respond to messages in your Inbox.

A co-worker sent you a message asking for feedback on a proposed agenda for an upcoming meeting. Unless you respond to him, he won't know what you think about the proposed agenda.

Reply Options

When you want to reply to a message, you have a few options.

- Use the *Reply* option to send a response to the sender of the message.
- Use the *Reply To All* option to send a response to the sender and copies of the response to anyone who received the original message.
- Use the *Forward* option to forward a copy of the message to someone who did not receive the original message.

The InfoBar

The InfoBar displays information about what has occurred or what action you need to take. It is displayed below the active toolbar. Figure 1-8 displays an example of the InfoBar.

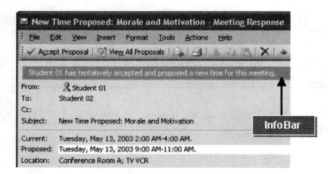

Figure 1-8: *An example of the InfoBar.*

How to Reply to a Message

Procedure Reference: Reply to a Message

To reply to an open message:

1. On the Standard toolbar, click Reply to display a Message form.

     The To and Subject text boxes are automatically filled in and information from the original message is inserted in the message body text box.

2. In the message body text box, enter the text of the message.

3. Send the message.

You don't have to open a message to reply to it. Simply select the message in the Inbox and, on the Standard toolbar, click Reply.

ACTIVITY 1-5

Replying to a Message

Setup:
The New Job Posting message is open.

Scenario:
The message from your co-worker contains the job description for the Technical Writer position. After reading the job description, you think it's perfect, and you actually have some candidates for the position. You need to inform your co-worker.

What You Do	How You Do It
1. Create a reply to the New Job Posting message.	a. On the Standard toolbar, click Reply ⟳ Reply .
	b. In the message body text box, **type** *The job description is perfect. I have some candidates for the position*.

2. When you create a reply to a message, the color of the reply text is _Blue_.

3. Send the message.	a. On the Standard toolbar, **click Send.**

4. After you send a reply, what is displayed in the InfoBar of the original message?

   a) Only the date you replied.

   b) Only the time you replied.

   c) The date and time you replied.

   d) The message "Your reply was sent."

5. Close the original message.	a. **Click the Close button** .

6. How does a message that you have replied to display in the Inbox?

   a) The header is bold.

   b) The header only contains an open envelope symbol.

   c) The header is not bold.

   d) The header contains an open envelope symbol with an arrow pointing left.

   e) The header contains an open envelope symbol with an arrow pointing right.

TOPIC F

Print a Message

Although an advantage of email is that it doesn't require paper, there will be occasions when you will want to have a hard copy of a message, either one you've sent or one you've received. In this topic, you will print a copy of a message.

A co-worker sent you the final meeting agenda in a message. Some of the agenda items are your responsibility. By printing a copy of the message, you will have a hard copy of the agenda for reference and portability, so you can easily prepare for the meeting.

How to Print a Message

Procedure Reference: Print a Message

To print a message:

1. Open the message you want to print.

2. Choose File→Print to display the Print dialog box.

3. To increase the number of copies you want to print, in the Number Of Copies spin box, click the up arrow as needed to enter the appropriate number of copies.

4. If necessary, modify the desired print options.

5. Click Print to print the message.

6. Close the message.

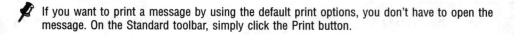 If you want to print a message by using the default print options, you don't have to open the message. On the Standard toolbar, simply click the Print button.

ACTIVITY 1-6

Printing a Message

Setup:
The contents of the Inbox are displayed. The New Job Posting message is selected.

Scenario:
The job description for the Technical Writer position is stored in your Inbox. You're going to be interviewing three candidates for the position, and you would like to distribute a copy of the description to each candidate.

What You Do	How You Do It
1. Open the New Job Posting message. Display the Print dialog box.	a. **Press Enter** to open the selected New Job Posting message.
	b. **Choose File→Print.**
2. The default number of copies is set to __ .	
3. The default page range is set to ___ .	
4. Print four copies of the message, and close the message.	a. In the Number Of Copies spin box, **click the up arrow three times** to enter the number 4.

Copies

Number of copies: 4

b. **Click Print.**

✎ If you are not connected to a printer, click Cancel to close the Print dialog box without printing the message.

c. **Choose File→Close.**

TOPIC G

Delete a Message

Once you start using Outlook to communicate electronically, your Inbox might fill up quickly with messages. In this topic, you will delete messages that you no longer need.

You have been using Outlook for a while, so your Inbox contains a lot of old messages that you no longer need. By deleting those old messages, your Inbox will be less cluttered and you will save space on your hard drive.

How to Delete a Message

Procedure Reference: Delete a Message

To delete a message:

1. With the message selected or opened that you want to delete, click the Delete button.

2. If necessary, verify the deletion of a message:

   a. In the All Mail Folders pane, click the plus sign (+) to expand your mailbox.

   b. Select the Deleted Items folder.

Recover Deleted Messages

After you delete a message, you can recover it from the Deleted Items folder.

- Drag the message from the Deleted Items folder to any other folder.

- Choose Edit→Undo Delete.

 This option only works immediately after deleting a message.

ACTIVITY 1-7

Deleting a Message

Setup:

The contents of the Inbox are displayed. The New Job Posting message is selected.

Scenario:

You have filled the Technical Writer position, so you no longer need the message that contains the job description.

What You Do	How You Do It
1. Delete the New Job Posting message.	a. On the Standard toolbar, **click the Delete button** ☒ .
2. Display the contents of the Deleted Items folder.	a. If necessary, in the All Mail Folders pane, **click the plus sign (+) to expand your mailbox.**
	b. **Select the Deleted Items folder.**
3. True or False? The New Job Posting message is displayed in the Deleted Items folder. ___ True ___ False	
4. Display the contents of the Inbox.	a. In the All Mail Folders pane, **select the Inbox.**

Lesson 1 Follow-up

Nice work! Now that you can identify the basic components of Outlook and you've sent and responded to email messages, you're ready to move ahead to the next step.

1. **What did you find most helpful about the Outlook environment? Why?**

2. **What did you find most confusing about the Outlook environment? Why?**

LESSON 2
Composing Messages

Lesson Objectives:

In this lesson, you will compose messages.

You will:

*   Address a message by using the Global Address List.
*   Format a message.
*   Check the spelling and grammar in a message.
*   Attach a file to a message.
*   Forward a message.

Introduction

You have created and responded to some basic messages. The longer you use Outlook, you will need to know how to create more detailed messages. In this lesson, you will create messages that include formatting, are error-free, and include information from other sources.

Before you send a message, you might find it necessary to alter its contents. Perhaps you want to emphasize some text within the body of the message or correct a misspelled word. Outlook provides you with tools to ensure that your messages are both accurate and easy to read.

TOPIC A

Address a Message

So far, you've sent mail messages where you knew the recipient's name and email address. What if you don't know the correct spelling of a person's name or their email address? In this topic, you will use an Outlook tool to accurately address email messages.

You need to send a get well card to a co-worker; however, you've forgotten her street address. Therefore, you use the phone book to ensure you have the correct address. Similar to a phone book, you can use an Outlook Address Book to quickly address an electronic message and ensure that the address of the recipient is correct.

Address Book

Definition:

The *Address Book* is a collection of address books or address lists that you can use to find and select names, email addresses, and distribution lists to quickly address messages.

Example:

Figure 2-1 displays an example of the Address Book.

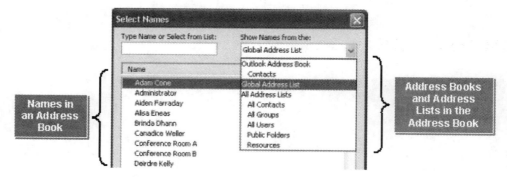

Figure 2-1: *An example of the Address Book.*

Global Address List

Definition:

The *Global Address List* is a list of all user names and global distribution lists in a particular organization that is created and maintained by the Microsoft Exchange Server Administrator. You can only access the Global Address List if you are using a Microsoft Exchange Server email account.

Example:

Figure 2-2 displays an example of a Global Address List.

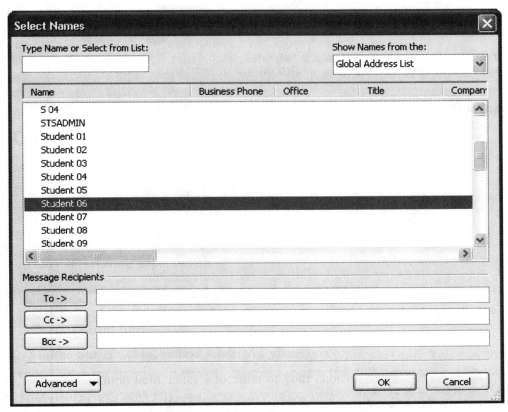

Figure 2-2: *The contents of a Global Address List.*

How to Address a Message

Procedure Reference: Address a Message

To address a message by using the Global Address List:

1. Display a new Message form.

2. To the left of the To text box, click To to display the Select Names dialog box.

3. In the list box, select the user name of the person to whom you want to address the message.

4. In the Message Recipients section, click To to place the selected user name in the To text box.

5. Click OK.

ACTIVITY 2-1

Addressing a Message

Objective:

To use the Global Address List to address a message.

Setup:

The contents of the Inbox are displayed.

Scenario:

You would like your co-worker to review a resume you received. You've forgotten how your co-worker spells her last name, so you're unsure of her email address.

What You Do	How You Do It
1. **Use the Global Address List to address a new message to your partner.**	a. **Display a new Message form.**
	b. To the left of the To text box, **click To** [To...] .
	c. In the list box of the Select Names dialog box, **select your partner's user name.**
	d. In the Message Recipients section, **click To** to place your partner's user name in the To text box.
	e. **Click OK.**
2. **Enter a subject of *Multimedia Developer Position*. Enter the text of the message.**	a. In the Subject text box, **type *Multimedia Developer Position***
	b. In the message body text box, **type *Attached is a resume for a candidate for the Multimedia Developer position. Most recently, she worked for Teknology, Inc. Let me know by tomorrow what you think.***
	c. **Press Enter twice.**
	d. **Type your name.**

TOPIC B

Format a Message

You have composed a message that contains text that you would like to make more distinctive. One way you can do that is to change the formatting of the text. In this topic, you will format a message.

You need to send a message that contains important dates and times for some upcoming events. You want to make sure that the dates and times stand out in the message text. By formatting specific text in a message, you will emphasize that text, drawing the reader's attention to it.

How to Format a Message

Procedure Reference: Format a Message

To format a message:

1. Select the text that you want to emphasize.

    🖈 To select all the message text, press Ctrl+A or choose Edit→Select All.

2. Apply the format.
    *   On the Standard toolbar, click the appropriate button.
    *   Choose Format and the appropriate formatting menu option.

ACTIVITY 2-2

Formatting a Message

Setup:
The Multimedia Developer Position message is open.

Scenario:
You want to emphasize specific message text so that it stands out from the rest of the message.

What You Do	How You Do It
1. **Apply bold formatting to the text tomorrow.**	a. **Select tomorrow.**
	b. On the Standard toolbar, **click the Bold button** **B** .

2. **The default font style of the message text is:**

a) Arial 12

b) Arial 10

c) Times New Roman 10

d) Times New Roman 12

---

3. **Change the font size of the message text to 12 and deselect the text.**

a. **Press Ctrl+A** to select the message text.

b. On the Standard toolbar, from the Font Size drop-down list, **select 12.**

c. **Click anywhere in the message body text** to deselect the message.

Topic C

Check Spelling and Grammar

Because the messages you already sent were basic, you weren't too worried about your spelling and grammar when you sent them. However, eventually, you will compose messages where accurate spelling and grammar will be essential. In this topic, you will check the spelling and grammar of a message.

Whenever you're typing, there's always the possibility of making an error. For example, you know the correct spelling of the word "their," but somehow it always comes out "thier" when you type it. When you are trying to convey a professional image, misspelled words and incorrect grammar can make you look unprofessional. With Outlook, you can ensure that there are no misspellings or incorrect grammar in your messages.

AutoCorrect

The AutoCorrect feature detects common typing mistakes, including misspelled words, grammar problems, incorrect capitalization, and common typos, and either automatically corrects them or brings them to your attention. By default, the AutoCorrect feature is on.

How to Check Spelling and Grammar

Procedure Reference: Check Spelling and Grammar

By default, spelling and grammar are automatically checked when you type a message. Wavy red underlines indicate a possible spelling error. Wavy green underlines indicate a possible error in grammar.

To check the spelling and grammar of a message all at once:

1. Choose Tools→Spelling And Grammar. The Spelling And Grammar dialog box is displayed.

    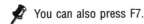 You can also press F7.

2. Correct any words that Outlook does not recognize.
    *   Click Ignore Once to skip the current occurrence of the word.
    *   Click Ignore All to skip all occurrences of the word.
    *   Click Add To Dictionary to keep the word unchanged and add the word to the user dictionary.
    *   Click Change after you change the spelling of the word by either entering a different spelling or selecting a word from the Suggestions list.
    *   Click Change All to change the spelling of all instances of the same word.

3. If a spelling and grammar error is found and corrected, click Yes to continue checking the remainder of the document.

4. Click OK to close the message box.

Recall a Message

You can recall, or take back, a sent message if the message meets the following criteria:
*   It has not been opened by the recipient.
*   It has not been moved from the Inbox.
*   The recipient is running Outlook and is logged on.

To recall a message:

1. Display the contents of the Sent Items folder.
2. Open the message you want to recall.
3. Choose Actions→Recall This Message.
4. In the Recall This Message dialog box, verify that Delete Unread Copies Of This Message is selected.
5. Click OK.
6. If you want to replace the message, create and send a new message.

ACTIVITY 2-3

Checking Spelling and Grammar

Setup:
The Multimedia Developer Position message is open and the message body text is selected.

Scenario:
Before you send the message to your co-worker, you want to make sure that it doesn't contain any spelling or grammar errors.

What You Do	How You Do It
1. True or False? The wavy red underline below the word Teknology indicates that there is a possible spelling error with the word. ___ True ___ False	
2. Check the spelling and grammar of the message, and correct any spelling errors as needed.	a. Choose Tools→Spelling And Grammar. b. When the word Teknology is selected as misspelled, **click Ignore All.** c. If necessary, **click Yes** to continue checking the remainder of the document. d. **Click OK** to close the message box.
3. True or False? After you correct any spelling errors, the word Teknology displays with the wavy red underline. ___ True ___ False	

TOPIC D

Attach a File

When you create a message, you might have information you want to include, but you don't want to retype that information in the message body. In this topic, you will attach a file to a message.

You have some information in a separate file that you want to include in a message. Retyping that information in the message will take some time. You can't copy and paste the information, because it's in a different file format. By attaching the file to your message, you can include the additional information without wasting time adding the information to your message.

Attachment

Definition:

An *attachment* is a copy of any type of file or an Outlook item that you can add to an Outlook item and then separate from the Outlook item.

Example:

Figure 2-3 displays an example of an attachment and the contents of the attachment in its associated application.

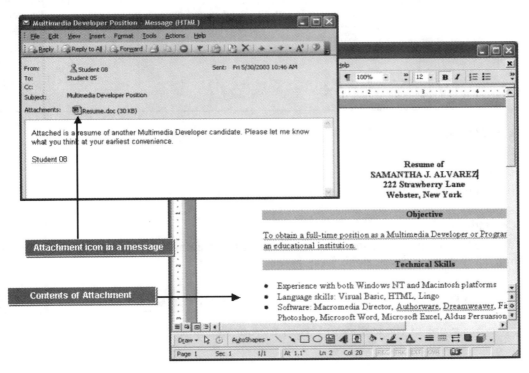

Figure 2-3: *An example of an attachment.*

File Type and Size

There are a few file type and size guidelines you should follow before attaching files or items to an Outlook item.

- Make sure the recipient of an attachment will be able to open and read the attachment. The recipient must have the application in which the attachment was created or a similar application.

- Be aware of attachment size, as a large attachment will use a lot of space and might delay the opening of the item to which it is attached.

How to Attach a File

Procedure Reference: Attach a File to a Message

To attach a file to a message:

1. On the E-mail toolbar, click the Insert File button. The Insert File dialog box is displayed.

2. Select the file you want to attach.
    - Double-click the file you want to attach.
    - Select the file you want to attach and click Insert.

    🖈 An attachment in a message that is formatted as HTML or Plain Text displays in a text box below the Subject text box. An attachment in a message that is formatted as Rich Text, or any other items, is included in the body of the item.

    🖈 After you send a message, sometimes the recipient has to wait a few moments for the message to display in the Inbox. To refresh the Inbox and display any incoming messages, you can click the Send/Receive button.

ACTIVITY 2-4

Attaching a File

Setup:
The Multimedia Developer Position message is open.

Scenario:
You need to include the candidate's resume with the email. The resume was created in another application to which you don't have access.

What You Do	How You Do It
1. What types of files will you attach to your messages?	

2. **Attach the resume to the message and send the message.**

   a. On the E-mail toolbar, **click the Insert File button** 📎 ▾.

   b. Using the Look In drop-down list, **display the contents of the 084680Data folder.**

   c. **Double-click the Resume file.**

   d. An Attach text box is added to the Message form. The file icon, name, and size appear in the Attach text box. **Send the message.**

3. **In the Inbox, how can you tell that a message contains an attachment?**

   a) The header contains the word Attachment.

   b) The header contains the word Attachment and an attachment symbol.

   c) An attachment symbol is displayed to the right of the subject text.

   d) The header doesn't contain any information to indicate that a message contains an attachment.

TOPIC E

Forward a Message

You have received messages and sent responses directly to the original sender of the message. But what if you want to send the message to someone who wasn't an original recipient? In this topic, you will forward a message.

You received a message from a co-worker that you want to share with another co-worker who didn't receive the original message. By forwarding the message, you can quickly and easily share the information. The only information that you need to enter is the recipient's email address.

How to Forward a Message

Procedure Reference: Forward a Message

To forward a message:

1. If necessary, open the message you want to forward.

2. On the Standard toolbar, click Forward. A new Message form is displayed.

3. Address the message to the appropriate recipients.

4. If desired, enter a message.

5. Send the message.

6. Close the original message.

ACTIVITY 2-5

Forwarding a Message

Setup:
The contents of the Inbox are displayed.

Scenario:
You want your manager's opinion on the qualifications of a candidate for the Multimedia Developer position. Your manager did not receive the original message that contained the candidate's resume, so he wants a copy of the message.

What You Do	How You Do It
1. Create a forward Message form for the Multimedia Developer Position message.	a. Open the Multimedia Developer Position message.
	b. On the Standard toolbar, **click Forward** to display a new Message form.

2. What text boxes in a forwarded Message form are prepopulated with text?

 a) To

 b) Cc

 c) Subject

 d) Attach

 e) Message body

3. In addition to the Subject text, what is displayed in the Subject text box of a message that indicates that the message will be or has been forwarded?

 a) FW:

 b) Forward:

 c) Frwd:

 d) Forwarded:

4. **Forward the message to your instructor and a copy to your partner. Close the original message.**

   a. In the To text box, **enter your instructor's user name.**

   b. In the Cc text box, **enter your partner's user name.**

   c. In the message body text box, **type *What do you think of this candidate?***

   d. **Send the message.**

   e. **Close the original message.**

Lesson 2 Follow-up

Congratulations! You've created several email messages by using a variety of options. The Global Address List will come in handy when you're not sure how to spell someone's name. You can make your messages look more professional by formatting them and checking their spelling and grammar. You will also be more efficient by attaching files and forwarding messages.

1. **Now that you know how to spell check an email message, do you think you will use that feature regularly? Why or why not?**

2. **What types of formatting do you think you will use in your email messages?**

NOTES

LESSON 3
Managing Mail

Lesson Time
50 minutes to 60 minutes

Lesson Objectives:

In this lesson, you will use folders to manage mail.

You will:

* Save an attachment.
* Flag a message.
* Create a folder.
* Move messages to a folder.
* Copy messages to multiple folders.
* Delete a folder.

Introduction

You have sent and received several messages, and your Inbox is starting to fill up. In this lesson, you will do some housekeeping to keep your messages organized and easier to find.

Your mailbox is overflowing. There are many messages you've received and want to keep yet others you no longer need. It's becoming more difficult to find certain messages. By organizing your mailbox, it will be easier to retrieve information efficiently.

TOPIC A

Open and Save an Attachment

You already know how to attach a file to a message and send it to someone. There will be times when you will receive a mail message that contains an attachment, and you will need to know what to do with the attached file. In this topic, you will save an attachment.

You received a message that contains an attachment. You have read the message, but you don't have time to review the contents of the attachment. By saving the attachment, you can refer to it later at a more convenient time. Also, you can then delete the message that you no longer need, saving space in your Inbox.

How to Open and Save an Attachment

Procedure Reference: Open an Attachment

To open an attachment:

1. Open the message that contains the attachment you want to open.

2. On the Attachments line of the Message form, double-click the name of the attachment to open the Opening Mail Attachment dialog box.

3. Click Open to open the file in the associated application. A message box is displayed.

4. Click OK to close the message box.

Procedure Reference: Save an Attachment

To save an attachment:

1. If necessary, open the message that contains the attachment you want to save.

2. Choose File→Save Attachments to display the Save Attachment dialog box.

3. If necessary, navigate to the folder location of your choice.

4. In the File Name text box, enter a name for the attachment.

5. Click Save.

6. Close the message.

> To delete an attachment, open the message that contains the attachment you want to delete. In the Attachments text box, select the attachment and click the Delete button.

ACTIVITY 3-1

Opening and Saving an Attachment

Data Files:

*   Resume.doc

Setup:

The Outlook window is maximized. The contents of the Inbox are displayed.

Scenario:

Your Inbox contains a number of messages with resumes as attachments. Whenever you need a resume, you're spending a lot of time trying to access the right one. It would be much easier if the resumes were in one place and the file name of each corresponded with the name on the resume.

What You Do	How You Do It
1. Open the file attached to the original Multimedia Developer Position message.	a. Open the original copy of the Multimedia Developer Position message.
	b. On the Attachments line of the Message form, **double-click the name of the attachment** to open it.

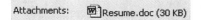

	c. The Opening Mail Attachment dialog box is displayed. **Click Open** to open the attachment.
	d. The file is opened in Microsoft Word. A message box is displayed. To close the message box and open the file in a new window, **click OK.**

2. True or False? The contents of the attachment include a resume for Samantha J. Alvarez.

___ True

___ False

3. Close the attachment.	a. In the Resume file window, **click the Microsoft Word Close button.**

4. Save a copy of the attachment in the My Documents folder as *Alvarez Resume* and close the message.

    a. Choose File→Save Attachments to display the Save Attachment dialog box.

    b. If necessary, **navigate to the My Documents folder.**

    c. In the File Name text box, **type *Alvarez Resume***

    d. **Click Save.**

    e. **Close the message.**

TOPIC B

Flag a Message

Some of the messages that you receive you will want to refer to later. By flagging a message, you can draw your attention to it. In this topic, you will flag a message.

You received a message that contains information that you will need to refer to in a few weeks. Because you have so many other messages in your Inbox, you're concerned that you will forget to revisit that particular message at the appropriate time. By flagging the message, it will stand out, drawing your attention to it. The flag will ensure that the message is easy to find and is a reminder to refer back to the message.

How to Flag a Message

Procedure Reference: Flag a Message for Follow-up

To flag a message for follow-up:

1. Right-click the message you want to flag and choose Follow Up→Add Reminder to display the Flag For Follow Up dialog box.

    📌 In an open message, you can click the Follow Up button on the Standard toolbar.

2. Click the Due By drop-down arrow. A pop-up Calendar is displayed.

3. Select the date on which you need to follow up.

4. Click OK.

    📌 When a flagged message is due for follow-up, the text in the message header will change from black to red.

5. If necessary, confirm that the message is marked for follow-up.

Mark a Message Unread

You can manually change the status of a message from read to unread.

1. In the Inbox, either select or open the message you want to mark as unread.
2. Choose Edit→Mark As Unread.

In the Inbox, the message is now bold and has a closed envelope symbol, indicating an unread message.

ACTIVITY 3-2

Flagging a Message

Objective:

To flag a message for follow-up.

Setup:

The Outlook window is maximized. The contents of the Inbox are displayed.

Scenario:

You've left a message for Samantha Alvarez. You're trying to schedule an interview with her. You don't want to forget to follow up with Samantha if you don't hear from her by the next business day.

What You Do	How You Do It
1. Flag the original Multimedia Developer Position message for follow-up tomorrow.	a. In the Inbox, **right-click the original Multimedia Developer Position message and choose Follow Up→Add Reminder.**
	b. The Flag For Follow Up dialog box is displayed. In the Due By drop-down list box, **click the drop-down arrow.**
	c. A pop-up Calendar is displayed. **Select the next business day.**
	d. **Click OK.**

2. After you flag a message for follow-up, how does it display in the Inbox?

   a) A red flag symbol is displayed to the left of the header.

   b) A green flag symbol is displayed to the right of the header.

   c) A green flag symbol is displayed to the left of the header.

   d) A blue flag symbol is displayed to the right of the header.

   e) A red flag symbol is displayed to the right of the header.

3. **Display the For Follow Up folder.**

a. In the Navigation Pane in the Favorite Folders pane, **click the For Follow Up folder.**

4. **True or False? The Multimedia Developer message you flagged for follow-up is displayed in the For Follow Up folder.**

    ___ True

    ___ False

5. **Display the contents of the Inbox.**

a. In the All Mail Folders pane, **select Inbox.**

TOPIC C

Create a Folder

Your Inbox contains many messages. It would be easier to find messages if they were stored in an organized manner. In this topic, you will create folders.

You have many messages in your Inbox that pertain to a variety of subjects. You need to re-read those messages that pertain to the upcoming job fair. It's going to take some time to locate all the messages you need. If your Inbox was organized so that all the messages that pertain to the job fair were together, your job would be so much easier.

How to Create a Folder

Procedure Reference: Create a Folder

To create a folder:

1. On the New Mail Message button, click the drop-down arrow. A drop-down menu is displayed.

2. From the expanded drop-down menu, choose Folder to display the Create New Folder dialog box.

3. In the Name text box, enter the name of the folder.

4. If necessary, in the Select Where To Place The Folder list box, select the location where you want to create the folder.

5. Click OK.

ACTIVITY 3-3

Creating a Folder

Setup:

The Outlook window is maximized. The contents of the Inbox are displayed.

Scenario:

Your Inbox is getting full. You want to keep some of the messages, but some of them you no longer need. You'd like to organize the messages in your Inbox, so it isn't so cluttered and it's easier to manage. You've received a number of messages that are related that you want to store together in one place.

What You Do	How You Do It
1. Create a folder in your Inbox named *Resumes*.	a. On the New Mail Message button, **click the drop-down arrow.**
	b. From the expanded drop-down menu, **choose Folder.**
	c. The Create New Folder dialog box is displayed. In the Name text box, **type** *Resumes*
	d. If necessary, in the Select Where To Place The Folder list box, **select Inbox.**
	e. **Click OK.**

2. True or False? In the All Mail Folders pane of the Navigation Pane, the Resumes folder is displayed below the Inbox.

    ___ True

    ___ False

3. In the Inbox, **create a** *Benefits* **and a** *Training* **folder.**

a. **Display the Create New Folder dialog box.**

b. **Name the folder** *Benefits*

c. **Place the folder in the Inbox.**

d. **Click OK.**

e. **Create a folder named** *Training* **in the Inbox.**

TOPIC D

Move Messages to a Folder

Your messages arrive in your Inbox, but they don't have to remain there. You created some new folders to better organize your messages. In this topic, you will transfer messages from one folder to another.

You created a folder to store all messages related to the job fair. Now, you need to move all the job fair messages to that new folder. After the messages are moved, your Inbox will be less cluttered and all the job fair messages will be in one place, easy to refer to when necessary.

How to Move Messages to a Folder

Procedure Reference: Move Messages to a Folder

To move messages to a folder:

1. Select the message you want to move.

2. On the Standard toolbar, click the Move To Folder button. A drop-down list is displayed.

3. Select the folder to which you want to move the message.

4. If necessary, in the All Mail Folders pane of the Navigation Pane, select the folder to which you moved the message to confirm that your message has been moved.

ACTIVITY 3-4

Moving Messages to a Folder

Setup:

The contents of the Inbox are displayed.

Scenario:

Your Inbox is full of various messages. Many of those messages contain resumes that could be stored in the Resumes folder.

What You Do	How You Do It
1. Move the original Multimedia Developer Position message to the Resumes folder.	a. Select the original Multimedia Developer Position message.
	b. On the Standard toolbar, **click the Move To Folder button** .
	c. From the drop-down list, **select Resumes.**
2. Display the contents of the Resumes folder, and display the contents of the Inbox.	a. In the All Mail Folders pane of the Navigation Pane, **select the Resumes folder.**
	b. In the All Mail Folders pane, **select Inbox.**

TOPIC E

Copy Messages to Folders

You might receive messages that contain information on more than one subject. It would make organizing more efficient if you could save those messages in more than one folder. In this topic, you will copy messages to multiple folders.

You received a message that contains information on two different subjects. Because the message refers to multiple subjects, you're not sure how to organize your Inbox so that you can find the information when you need it. By copying the message, the information it contains can be stored in multiple folders with other similar information.

How to Copy Messages to a Folder

Procedure Reference: Copy Messages to a Folder

To copy a message to a folder:

1. Select the message you want to copy.

2. Choose Edit→Copy.

3. In the All Mail Folders pane, select the folder to which you want to copy the message.

4. Choose Edit→Paste to paste the copied message to the selected folder.

ACTIVITY 3-5

Copying Messages to Folders

Objective:

To move the System Training message to the Training folder and then copy the message to the Benefits folder.

Data Files:

• System Training.msg

Setup:

The contents of the Inbox are displayed.

Scenario:

You received a message that includes information on two different subjects. You want to make sure that the message is stored appropriately so that it's easy to find the information when you need to refer to it.

What You Do	How You Do It
1. Open the System Training message.	a. Double-click the System Training message.

2. What information does the System Training message contain?

    a) Information on system training only.

    b) Information on system training and vacation.

    c) Information on system training and health insurance.

    d) Information on system training and retirement plans.

3. Close the message, move the System Training message to the Training folder, and display the contents of the Training folder.

    a. Click the Close button.

    b. On the Standard Toolbar, click the Move To Folder button and choose Training.

    c. Open the Training folder.

4. Copy the System Training message to the Benefits folder.

    a. Choose Edit→Copy.

    b. Select the Benefits folder.

    c. Choose Edit→Paste.

TOPIC F

Delete a Folder

Inboxes tend to fill up very quickly with messages and folders. Before you know it, you have dozens of old items that you no longer need. In this topic, you will delete folders.

You created a folder to store the messages for a particular project. The project is complete and you no longer need the folder or its contents. By deleting the folder, you will save space and your Inbox will be easier to manage because it won't contain unnecessary information.

How to Delete a Folder

Procedure Reference: Delete a Folder

To delete a folder:

1. In the All Mail Folders pane, select the folder you want to delete.

2. On the Standard toolbar, click the Delete button.

3. In the message box, click Yes to confirm the deletion of the selected folder.

ACTIVITY 3-6

Deleting a Folder

Setup:
The contents of the Benefits folder are displayed.

Scenario:
You have messages and folders that you no longer need.

What You Do	How You Do It
1. **Delete the Resumes folder.**	a. In the All Mail Folders pane, **select the Resumes folder.**
	⚠ Make sure you've selected the folder.
	b. On the Standard toolbar, **click the Delete button.**
	c. In the message box, **click Yes** to confirm the deletion of the Resumes folder.

2. **True or False? In the All Mail Folders pane, the Deleted Items folder indicates that it contains items.**
   ___ True
   ___ False

Lesson 3 Follow-up

Congratulations! You now know how to keep your mailbox organized so that you can access and retrieve messages efficiently. You know how to work with attachments and flag messages for easy reference. You can create folders and move and copy messages to suit your needs. In addition, you can also delete folders that are no longer needed.

1. **List some reasons you might flag a message.**

2. **What folders could you create to better organize your messages?**

LESSON 4
Scheduling Appointments

Lesson Time
30 minutes to 40 minutes

Lesson Objectives:

In this lesson, you will schedule appointments.

You will:

- List the components of the Outlook Calendar.
- Schedule an appointment.
- Assign a category to an appointment.
- Update Calendar entries.

Introduction

You have discovered how Outlook helps you communicate electronically and manage those communications. You can also keep your schedule organized electronically by using the Calendar. In this lesson, you will use the Calendar to manage your appointments.

Your paper calendar is a mess. You've scheduled, rescheduled, and cancelled appointments. There are scribbled notes posted on certain days as reminders. By using the Outlook Calendar, your schedule will always be up to date and easy to read.

TOPIC A

The Outlook Calendar

Before you use the Calendar, you will need to become familiar with its components and how they work. By understanding the basics of the Calendar, you will have a solid foundation upon which to build more critical skills. In this topic, you will explore the Outlook Calendar and identify its components.

After logging on to Outlook for the first time, you familiarized yourself with the Outlook environment. Before using the Calendar, it's important to familiarize yourself with it. By knowing the components of the Calendar, it will be easier to use and you will be able to work more efficiently because you are familiar with it.

Calendar Entries

There are different types of entries that you can create in your Calendar. Those entry types are listed in the following table.

Entry Type	Used To
Appointment	Reserve a time slot once for a designated purpose.
Recurring Appointment	Reserve a time slot more than once for a designated purpose.
Event	Reserve a specific day or group of days for a designated purpose.
Meeting Request	Reserve a time slot once for a designated purpose involving other participants.
Recurring Meeting Request	Reserve a time slot more than once for a designated purpose involving other participants.

Views

Definition:

    A *view* is a way to display items in an Outlook folder.

Example:

Figure 4-1 displays an example of a Calendar view.

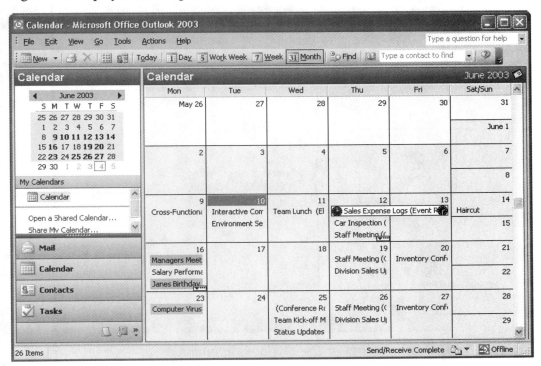

Figure 4-1: *An example of the Month view.*

Calendar Views

Items on your Calendar can be viewed in several ways. The most common Calendar views are listed in the following table.

View	Displays
Day	A detailed schedule for one day, divided in hourly time slots.
Work Week	The five work days (Monday through Friday) divided in hourly time slots.
Week	The entire week (Monday through Sunday) where each day is represented by a box with no time slots.
Month	An entire month with no time slots.

The Outlook Calendar

The Calendar consists of two main components.

- The *Appointment Section* is divided into hourly time slots and displays all appointments for that day.
- The *Date Navigator* consists of Calendars for two adjacent months that you can use to quickly select a date to display or add items.

Figure 4-2 displays the components of the Outlook Calendar.

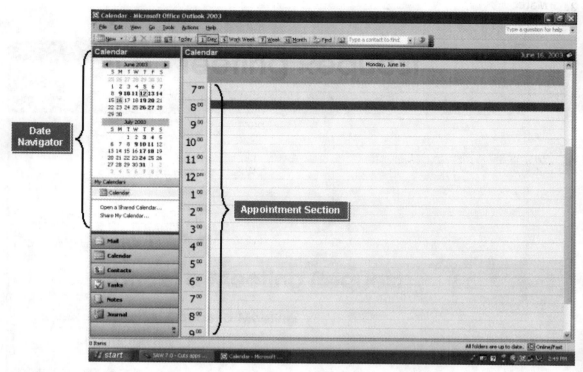

Figure 4-2: *The components of the Outlook Calendar.*

ACTIVITY 4-1

Exploring the Outlook Calendar

Setup:

The Inbox is displayed.

Scenario:

Before you can begin using the Calendar efficiently, it's a good idea to spend some time familiarizing yourself with the Calendar environment.

What You Do	How You Do It
1. **Display the Calendar.**	a. In the Navigation Pane on the Go Menu, select **Calendar**. 

2. **Match the types of Calendar entries with their corresponding definitions.**

____ Appointment

____ Event

____ Meeting

a. Appointment that involves scheduling with other participants and resources.

b. Activity that is associated with a specific day (or group of days) and a year, but not with a specific time.

c. Reservation of a time slot for a designated purpose.

---

3. **Display the different Calendar views.**

a. On the Standard toolbar, **click Work Week** `5 Work Week` .

b. The current week, Monday through Friday, is displayed with time slots. On the Standard toolbar, **click Week** `7 Week` .

c. The current week, Monday through Sunday, is displayed without time slots. On the Standard toolbar, **click Month** `31 Month` . The current month is displayed, without time slots.

d. On the Standard toolbar, **click Day** `1 Day` to return to the current day.

TOPIC B

Schedule an Appointment

You have used paper calendars to keep track of your schedule. Your Outlook Calendar allows you to perform the same functions as a paper calendar and more. In this topic, you will add an appointment to your Outlook Calendar.

A new client invites you to discuss their first project over lunch tomorrow. You accept the invitation, but you don't bother writing it down because you're sure you'll remember it. When you return from lunch the next day, you find a note on your desk from your manager asking you why you didn't show up for a meeting you had agreed to with him. How could you forget the meeting? By using the Outlook Calendar to track your time, you can avoid this type of predicament in the future.

The Appointment Form

When you create a new appointment, Outlook displays an Appointment form that contains text boxes in which you can enter specific information. Some of the text boxes in an Appointment form are listed in Table 4-1.

Table 4-1: *Appointment Form Text Boxes*

Text Box	Information to Enter
Subject	A brief description of the appointment.
Location	Where the appointment will be held.
Start Time	The date and time the appointment starts.
End Time	The date and time the appointment ends.
Reminder	A reminder that notifies you when it's almost time for the appointment.
Show Time As	How the appointment should be displayed on your Calendar.
Label	What type of appointment it is.
Message Area	A place to enter any additional information about the appointment.

Figure 4-3 displays an example of a completed Appointment form.

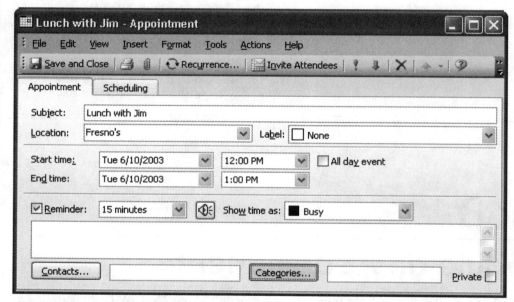

Figure 4-3: *A completed Appointment form.*

Calendar Symbols

To make it easier to determine at a glance what is on your Calendar, items on your Calendar are displayed with symbols.

Examples of Message Symbols

Some frequently used symbols are listed in Table 4-2.

Table 4-2: *Symbols Used in the Outlook Calendar*

Symbol	Meaning
☼	This appointment has a reminder.
↻	This is a recurring appointment.

Symbol	Meaning
◫	This is a meeting that involves multiple participants.

How to Schedule an Appointment

Procedure Reference: Schedule an Appointment

To schedule an appointment:

1. In the Date Navigator, select the date of the appointment.

    You can also select the date and time in the Appointment form.

2. On the Standard toolbar, click the New Appointment button to display a new Appointment form.

3. In the Subject field, enter a subject of your choice.

4. Press Tab to move to the Location field.

5. In the Location field, enter a location of your choice.

6. From the Start Time drop-down list, select the appropriate starting time of the appointment.

7. From the End Time drop-down list, select the appropriate ending time of the appointment.

8. Save and close the appointment.

Appointment Reminders

An appointment reminder is a visual and auditory alarm notifying you that you have an appointment. By default, each scheduled appointment has a reminder of 15 minutes.

ACTIVITY 4-2

Scheduling an Appointment

Setup:

The current day is displayed in the Calendar.

Scenario:

You just made plans with Jim for lunch at Fresno's one week from today from 12 PM to 1 PM. In addition, you just scheduled an appointment for a haircut this Saturday from 1 PM to 2 PM.

What You Do	How You Do It
1. Display a new Appointment form for one week from today.	a. On the Date Navigator, **click the date one week from today.**
	b. On the Standard toolbar, **click the New Appointment button** `New ▾` .
2. Enter a subject of *Lunch with Jim* and the location, *Fresno's*.	a. In the Subject field, **type** *Lunch with Jim*
	b. **Press Tab.**
	c. **Type** *Fresno's*
3. Set the time of the appointment from 12 to 1 PM.	a. **Click the Start Time drop-down arrow.**
	Start time: Wed 5/14/2003 ▾ 8:00 AM ▾
	End time: Wed 5/14/2003 ▾ 8:30 AM ▾
	b. **Scroll to select 12:00 PM.**
	c. From the End Time drop-down list, **select 1:00 PM (1 hour).**
4. The default reminder for an appointment is:	
a) 5 minutes	
b) 10 minutes	
c) 15 minutes	
d) 20 minutes	
5. Save the appointment.	a. On the Standard toolbar, **click Save And Close.**

6. **What does the symbol that is displayed with the new appointment indicate?**

   a) The appointment is recurring.

   b) The appointment has a reminder.

   c) The appointment is private.

---

7. **Create an appointment for a haircut this Saturday from 1 PM to 2 PM.**

   a. In the Date Navigator, **select this Saturday's date.**

   b. **Display a new Appointment form.**

   c. **Enter the subject of** *Haircut*

   d. **Set the appointment starting time to 1 PM.**

   e. **Set the appointment ending time to 2 PM.**

   f. **Save and close the appointment.**

Procedure Reference: Create a Recurring Appointment

To create a recurring appointment:

1. In the Date Navigator, select the date of the appointment.

2. On the Standard toolbar, click the New Appointment button to display a new Appointment form.

3. In the Subject field, enter a subject of your choice.

4. In the Location field, enter a location of your choice.

5. From the Start Time drop-down list, select the appropriate starting time of the appointment.

6. From the End Time drop-down list, select the appropriate ending time of the appointment.

7. On the Standard toolbar, click Recurrence to display the Appointment Recurrence dialog box.

8. If necessary, in the Recurrence Pattern box, select the recurrence pattern.

9. If necessary, in the Range Of Recurrence box, select the range of recurrence.

10. Click OK to close the dialog box and return to the Appointment form.

11. Save and close the appointment.

ACTIVITY 4-3

Creating a Recurring Appointment

Setup:

This Saturday's date is displayed in the Calendar.

Scenario:

You've been assigned to a special project team. One of the team members works in another location. For the next six weeks, you will meet with the team on a weekly basis on Friday from 10 AM to 11 AM. During the meeting, you will call the off-site team member so you can include him in the project meetings.

What You Do	How You Do It
1. **Create a new appointment for the upcoming Friday with a subject of *Inventory Conference Call* and a starting time of 10 AM.**	a. **Display the upcoming Friday's date.**
	b. **Display a new Appointment form.**
	c. **Enter a subject of *Inventory Conference Call***
	d. **Enter a starting time of 10 AM.**
	e. **Enter an ending time of 11 AM.**
2. **Set the recurrence options so that the appointment occurs on a weekly basis for six weeks.**	a. **On the Standard toolbar, click Recurrence** [🔁 Recurrence...] **.**
	b. **In the Range Of Recurrence box, select the End After option, press Tab, and type *6***
	○ No end date ⊙ End after: [6] occurrences
	c. **Click OK to return to the Appointment form.**

3. **How is the Appointment form different after you set the recurrence options?**

   a) The InfoBar indicates the day of the week, the dates the meeting will occur, and at what time.

   b) The title bar indicates that the appointment is now recurring.

   c) The Starting Time and Ending Time fields are no longer displayed.

   d) The reminder is now set to 30 minutes.

   e) The InfoBar indicates the dates of the meetings only.

4. **Save and close the appointment.**

5. **What do the symbols that are displayed with the appointment indicate?**

   a) The appointment has a reminder only.

   b) The appointment is private.

   c) The appointment is recurring only.

   d) The appointment has a reminder and is recurring.

6. **View the recurring appointment by using the Month view and then return to the Day view.**

   a. **Display the current month.**

   b. **Click the Day button.**

Procedure Reference: Create an Event

To create an event:

1. In the Date Navigator, select the date of the appointment.

2. On the Standard toolbar, click the New Appointment button to display a new Appointment form.

3. In the Subject field, enter a subject of your choice.

4. In the Location field, enter a location of your choice.

5. Check the All Day Event check box.

6. From the End Time drop-down list, select the appropriate ending time of the appointment.

7. From the Show Time As drop-down list, select the desired option.

8. Save and close the appointment.

ACTIVITY 4-4

Creating an Event

Setup:
The Day view is displayed in the Calendar.

Scenario:
You have a two-day Microsoft Office 2003 training seminar to attend starting two weeks from the upcoming Wednesday. It's an all-day event and will be held at the Royal Suites. You want to make sure that someone viewing your Calendar will know that you are not available during that time.

What You Do	How You Do It
1. Display a new Appointment form for the appropriate date.	a. Display the date two weeks from the upcoming Wednesday.
	b. Display a new Appointment form.
2. Enter the subject and location of the event.	a. In the Subject text box, **type *Microsoft Office 2003 Training***
	b. In the Location text box, **type *Royal Suites***

3. **Change the appointment to an all-day event, select an end date, show the time as out of office, and save and close the form.**

a. **Check the All Day Event check box.**

☐ All day event

b. **Click the End Time drop-down arrow.**

c. **Select the end date.**

d. **From the Show Time As drop-down list, select Out Of Office.**

e. **Click Save And Close.**

4. **True or False? Events do not occupy blocks of time in your Calendar.**

___ True

___ False

5. **Events appear in _____ at the top of the date(s) you specified in the Calendar.**

6. **In addition to the banner at the top of the Appointment Section, how is the training event represented in your Calendar?**

a) A purple banner is displayed on the specified dates.

b) A white banner is displayed on the specified dates.

c) A blue banner is displayed on the specified dates.

d) A green banner is displayed on the specified dates.

7. **Display the current day.**

a. On the Standard toolbar, **click the Go To Today button** [Today] to display today's date only.

TOPIC C

Assign a Category to an Appointment

You have added several business and personal appointments to your Calendar. It would be great if there was a way to quickly identify which appointments were the most important. In this topic, you will assign a category to an appointment.

Your Calendar contains some appointments that you don't want to miss, such as your performance appraisal. It also contains some appointments that you would like to miss, such as lunch with your co-worker whom you despise. By organizing your appointments so that similar appointments are grouped together, it will be easy to identify the appointments you don't want to miss.

Category

Definition:

A *category* is a keyword or phrase that you can assign to related items so that you can easily track the items.

Example:

Figure 4-4 displays an example of default categories in Outlook.

Figure 4-4: *The default categories.*

How to Assign a Category to an Appointment

Procedure Reference: Assign a Category to an Existing Appointment

To assign a category to an existing appointment:

📌 You can assign a category while you're creating an appointment.

1. Open the appointment to which you want to assign a category.
    *   Double-click the appointment.
    *   Right-click the appointment and choose Open.
    *   Select the appointment and choose File→Open→Selected Items.

2. Click Categories to display the Categories dialog box.

3. In the Available Categories list box, check the category to which you want to assign the appointment.

4. Click OK.

5. Save and close the appointment.

Procedure Reference: Assign a Category to a Recurring Appointment

To assign a category to a recurring appointment:

1. Open the appointment to which you want to assign a category.
    *   Double-click the appointment.
    *   Right-click the appointment and choose Open.
    *   Select the appointment and choose File→Open→Selected Items.

2. In the Open Recurring Item dialog box, click OK.

3. Click Categories to display the Categories dialog box.

4. In the Available Categories list box, check the category to which you want to assign the appointment.

5. Click OK.

6. Save and close the appointment.

ACTIVITY 4-5

Assigning a Category to an Appointment

Objective:

To assign a category to an existing appointment.

Setup:

The current date is displayed in the Calendar.

Scenario:

You want to be able to display similar appointments together in the Calendar, so that at a glance you can identify those appointments.

What You Do	How You Do It
1. Assign the Personal category to the Lunch with Jim appointment.	a. **Display the date one week from today.** b. **Double-click the Lunch with Jim Appointment form.** c. **Click Categories to display the Categories dialog box.** d. **In the Available Categories list box, check Personal.** 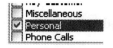 e. **Click OK.**  f. **Save and close the Appointment form.**
2. Assign the Business category to the Inventory Conference Call appointments.	a. **Display the upcoming Friday's date.**

b. **Double-click the Inventory Conference Call appointment.**

c. In the Open Recurring Item dialog box, **select Open The Series.**

d. **Click OK** to display the Recurring Appointment form.

e. **Display the Categories dialog box.**

f. **Check Business.**

g. **Click OK.**

h. **Save and close the Appointment form.**

3. **Display the appointments by category, and return the Calendar to Day view.**

a. **Choose View→Arrange By→Current View→By Category.**

b. If necessary, **expand the Business category** to display the Inventory Conference Call appointment.

c. If necessary, **expand the Personal category** to display the Lunch with Jim appointment.

d. To return the Calendar to Day view, **choose View→Arrange By→Current View→Day/Week/Month.**

TOPIC D

Update Calendar Entries

You have just scheduled some appointments in your Calendar. What if the date, time, or location of an appointment changes? In this topic, you will update Calendar entries.

It never fails—the minute you schedule an appointment, you learn about another one you have to attend that's scheduled for the same time. When you're done crossing out, filling in, whiting out, or erasing your appointment information, your paper-based calendar is a mess. By using the Outlook Calendar, you can throw away your eraser and correction fluid. Updating your Calendar is a breeze, and your Calendar remains neat and organized, ensuring accurate appointment information.

How to Update Calendar Entries

Procedure Reference: Edit Appointments

To edit an appointment:

1. Open the Appointment form of the appointment that you want to edit.

2. Make the appropriate edits in the Appointment form.

3. Click Save And Close.

Delete Appointments

There are a few options for deleting an appointment. To delete an appointment, you can:

- Right-click the appointment and choose Delete.

- Select the appointment and on the Standard toolbar, click the Delete button.

- Open the appointment and on the Standard toolbar, click the Delete button.

ACTIVITY 4-6

Updating Calendar Entries

Setup:

The current date is displayed in the Calendar.

Scenario:

Jim called to tell you that he can't do lunch next week from 12–1 PM. He would like to meet from 1:30 PM to 2:30 PM instead.

What You Do	How You Do It
1. Why might you need to update a Calendar entry?	
2. Change the Lunch with Jim appointment time to 1:30 PM to 2:30 PM.	a. Display the date one week from today.
	b. Display the Lunch with Jim Appointment form.
	c. Change the start time to 1:30 PM.
3. When you entered a new start time, what happened to the end time?	
a) It stayed the same.	
b) It automatically changed to 2:00 PM.	
c) It automatically changed to 2:30 PM.	
d) None of these.	
4. Save and close the Appointment form.	

Lesson 4 Follow-up

Nice work! Now you know how to use the Calendar to keep track of all your appointments and events. You can schedule an appointment at a specified time, assign a category to an appointment, and update Calendar entries. Now your schedule will always be up-to-date and easy to read.

1. What are some functions that you can perform by using the Outlook Calendar that you cannot perform with a paper-based calendar?

2. When scheduling appointments, will you use categories? Why or why not?

LESSON 5
Scheduling Meetings

Lesson Time
60 minutes to 70 minutes

Lesson Objectives:

In this lesson, you will schedule meetings.

You will:

- Schedule a meeting.
- Reply to a meeting request.
- Propose a new meeting time.
- Track meeting responses.
- Update a meeting request.
- Cancel a meeting request.
- Print the Calendar.

Introduction

You have used the Inbox to send messages and the Calendar to track your important appointments. In this lesson, you will combine these two tasks to schedule and coordinate meetings that involve multiple participants.

You need to schedule a department meeting. You must notify all employees, reserve a slide projector, and determine who will be attending. By using Outlook, you can electronically communicate and track attendance of participants and resources at meetings from one central location.

TOPIC A

Schedule a Meeting

When you scheduled appointments that involved your schedule only, all you had to do was enter the information in your Calendar. Now, you will combine two of the tasks you've already learned—sending mail messages and scheduling appointments—to schedule meetings that involve multiple participants.

You need to schedule a department meeting. You could invite the participants by phone, but that will take some time, especially if someone is not available at the designated time. By scheduling a meeting in Outlook, you can quickly invite the appropriate participants and resources all at the same time, and you can pick a time that is available for everyone.

The Meeting Scheduling Process

The process begins with a Meeting form that you complete and send to all the meeting participants. The meeting is scheduled on your Calendar as soon as you send the Meeting form. As each participant accepts or tentatively accepts the meeting, it is inserted on their Calendar, and a response is sent to the meeting organizer. If the meeting is declined or a new time is proposed, a reply is sent. Figure 5-1 displays the meeting scheduling process.

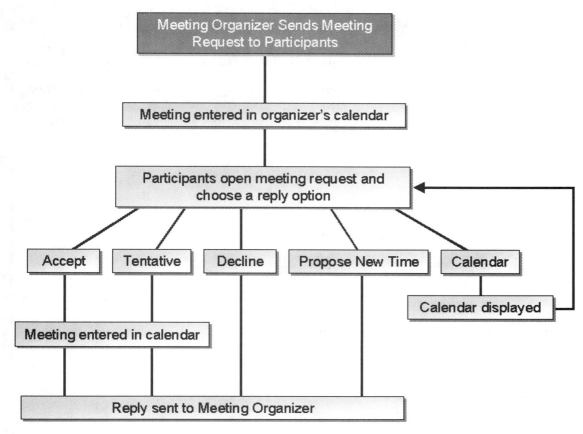

Figure 5-1: *The meeting scheduling process.*

The Meeting Form

The Meeting form is used to invite participants to a meeting. It consists of three tabs:

- The *Appointment* tab allows you to enter a subject, a location for the meeting, start and end times, and any other information regarding the meeting.

- The *Scheduling* tab allows you to coordinate the meeting to fit the schedules of all attendees.

- The *Tracking* tab displays the meeting participants and their replies. This section is not visible until the Meeting form is sent to the participants.

Figure 5-2 displays an example of a completed Meeting form.

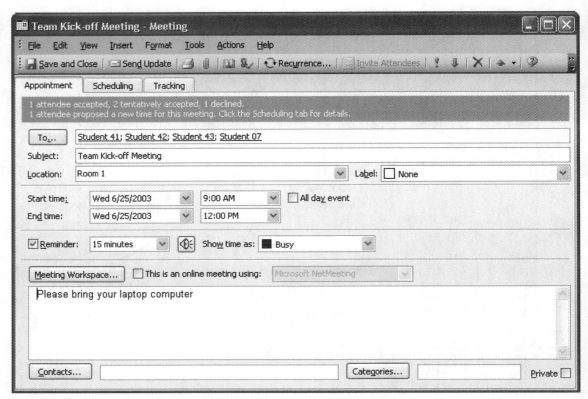

Figure 5-2: *A completed Meeting form.*

Meeting Resources

Definition:

A *meeting resource* is an item with its own email account on the Microsoft Exchange Server that you can schedule for a meeting, and it will automatically accept or reject meeting invitations.

Example:

Figure 5-3 displays examples of meeting resources in the Global Address List.

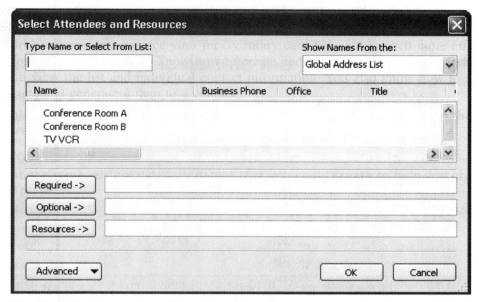

Figure 5-3: *Examples of meeting resources.*

How to Schedule a Meeting

Procedure Reference: Schedule a Meeting

To schedule a meeting:

1. In the Date Navigator, select the date of the meeting.

2. In the Appointment section, click the time you want the meeting to start.

   🖈 You can also select the date and time in the Meeting form.

3. On the Standard toolbar, click the New Appointment button drop-down arrow and choose Meeting Request to display a new Meeting form.

4. To address the request by using the Global Address List, click To to display the Select Attendees And Resources dialog box.

   🖈 You can also type the user names of the attendees directly in the To text box, separating each user name with a semicolon (;).

5. In the list box, select the appropriate attendees.

6. Click Required to add the selected user names to the Required text box.

7. If necessary, in the list box, select the appropriate resources.

8. If necessary, click Resources to add the selected resources to the Resources text box.

9. Click OK to return to the Meeting form.

10. In the Subject text box, enter a meeting subject.

11. If necessary, from the End Time drop-down list, select an end time for the meeting.

12. To check the availability of the attendees, select the Scheduling tab.

13. On the Standard toolbar, click Send to send the meeting request.

Online Meetings

To schedule an online meeting:

1. Open and complete a Meeting form as you would if you were scheduling an in-person meeting.

2. Check the This Is An Online Meeting Using check box and from the accompanying drop-down list, select one of the options.
   - Microsoft NetMeeting
   - Windows Media Services
   - Microsoft Exchange Conferencing

3. If you are using Microsoft NetMeeting, in the Directory Server text box, enter the name of the server you are using.

4. If you are using Windows Media Services, in the Event Address text box, enter the address of the event.

5. If you are using Microsoft Exchange Conferencing:
   - If you want to create a private meeting, uncheck the Allow External Attendees Or Users Without Trusted User Certificates To Join The Conference check box.
   - If you want to require a password for those entering the meeting, in the Password text box, enter a password.

6. If you want a Microsoft NetMeeting or a Windows Media Services broadcast to start automatically, check the appropriate option.
   - Automatically Start NetMeeting With Reminder
   - Automatically Start Windows Media With Reminder

7. Click Send.

ACTIVITY 5-1

Scheduling a Meeting

Setup:
The Calendar is displayed.

Scenario:
At the last managers' meeting, the issue of new vacation policy was discussed. The managers need to meet with their staff to discuss possible options for a new vacation policy and request input. You are available one week from the upcoming Tuesday. You should allow two hours for the meeting. You will need the TV VCR. You believe Conference Room A will accommodate the attendees.

What You Do	How You Do It
1. Display a Meeting form for the date one week from the upcoming Tuesday at 2:00 PM.	a. In the Date Navigator, **select the date one week from the upcoming Tuesday.**
	b. In the Appointment section, **click 2:00 PM.**
	c. On the Standard toolbar, **click the New Appointment button drop-down arrow and choose Meeting Request.**
2. Using the Global Address List, **address the message to your partner.**	a. In the Meeting form, **click To.**
	b. In the list box of the Select Attendees And Resources dialog box, **select your partner's user name.**
	c. **Click Required** to place the selected user names in the Required text box.
3. Reserve Conference Room A and the TV VCR.	a. In the list box, **select Conference Room A and the TV VCR.**
	b. **Click Resources** to place the selected resources in the Resources text box.
	c. **Click OK** to return to the Meeting form.

4. The subject is *Vacation Policy*, and change the end time to 4:00 PM. Display the Scheduling tab.

    a. In the Subject text box, **type *Vacation Policy***

    b. If necessary, from the End Time drop-down list, **select 4:00 PM (2 hours).**

    c. **Select the Scheduling tab.**

5. **Are Conference Room A and the TV VCR listed with the other meeting attendees?**

6. **Send the meeting request.**

    a. On the Standard toolbar, **click Send.**

TOPIC B

Reply to a Meeting Request

You know how to schedule a meeting and invite participants to your meeting. But how do you respond to an invitation to someone else's meeting? In this topic, you will reply to a meeting request.

You received a meeting invitation from a co-worker. You could call her and tell her that you will be attending, but what if she (or you) forgets to document your participation? By using Outlook to reply to a meeting request, the meeting chairperson will be assured of your attendance. Therefore, you won't have to worry about showing up for a meeting at which your attendance isn't expected. Also, you won't forget about the meeting because it will be documented on your electronic Calendar.

How to Reply to a Meeting Request

Procedure Reference: Reply to a Meeting Request

To accept or decline a meeting request:

1. In the Inbox, open the meeting request message.

2. If desired, on the Standard toolbar, click Calendar to check your Calendar.

3. If necessary, click the Close button to close the Calendar.

4. Accept or decline a meeting request.
   - To accept the meeting request.
   a. On the Standard toolbar, click Accept.
   b. In the message box, click OK to send the response.

   You could choose to edit the response before sending or accept without sending a response.

- To decline the meeting request.
  a. On the Standard toolbar, click Decline. A message box is displayed.
  b. Click OK to edit the response before sending.
  c. In the message area of the response form, type a response.
  d. Click OK.

🖈 You could choose to send the response without editing it or decline without sending a response.

5. Click Send.

Meeting Conflicts

When you open a meeting request for a meeting that conflicts with another appointment on your Calendar, Outlook alerts you by displaying a warning in the InfoBar. Conflicting meetings are displayed adjacent to each other on the Calendar.

ACTIVITY 5-2

Replying to a Meeting Request

Objective:
To accept and decline meeting requests.

Setup:
The date one week from the upcoming Tuesday is displayed in the Calendar. Your assigned partner is also performing this activity, and you have decided who is User A and who is User B.

Scenario:
Because you work with more than one department, you received more than one meeting request for the Vacation Policy meeting. You can attend only one of the meetings.

LESSON 5

What You Do	How You Do It

User A

1. From one of the Vacation Policy meeting requests in your Inbox, **check your Calendar and accept the meeting.**

   a. **Display the Inbox.**

   b. **Open one of the Vacation Policy meeting requests.**

   c. The InfoBar indicates that this meeting request conflicts with another appointment on your Calendar. To view your schedule for the day of the meeting, on the Standard toolbar, **click Calendar** 🔍 Calendar... .

   d. **Click the Close button.**

   e. On the Standard toolbar, **click Accept** ✓ Accept .

   f. To send the response now, **click OK.**

   g. If necessary, **close any open Message forms.**

User B

2. **Decline one of the other Vacation Policy meetings stating that you have another meeting scheduled for that time.**

   a. **Display the Inbox.**

   b. If necessary, **open one of the other Vacation Policy meeting requests.**

   c. On the Standard toolbar, **click Decline** ✕ Decline .

   d. To accept the default response to edit the response before sending, **click OK.**

   e. In the message body text box, **type** *Sorry—I have another meeting scheduled for the same time*.

   f. **Click Send.**

TOPIC C

Propose a New Meeting Time

You have seen how to accept and decline a meeting request. However, what if you need to attend a meeting but are not available at the requested date or time? In this topic, you will discover how to propose a new meeting time.

You received an invitation to a meeting which you need to attend, but you are not available at the scheduled time. You could decline the invitation and compose a new message suggesting an alternate meeting time and requesting the meeting chairperson's reply; however, that will take some time and possibly a lot of emails. To save time, you could propose a new time for the meeting.

How to Propose a New Meeting Time

Procedure Reference: Propose a New Meeting Time

To propose a new meeting time:

1. In the Inbox, open the meeting request message.

2. On the Standard toolbar, click Propose New Time to display the Propose New Time dialog box.

3. From the Meeting Start Time drop-down list, select a new time.

4. Click Propose Time to display the Meeting Response form.

5. In the message text box, enter a response.

6. Click Send.

ACTIVITY 5-3

Proposing a New Meeting Time

Setup:

The Inbox is displayed.

Scenario:

You would like to attend the remaining meeting request, but it obviously conflicts with your schedule. You're wondering if the meeting time can be changed.

What You Do	How You Do It
1. For the remaining meeting request, send a reply to the meeting organizer proposing that the meeting run from 9:00 AM to 11:00 AM.	a. Open the remaining Vacation Policy meeting request.
	b. On the Standard toolbar, **click Propose New Time** [Propose New Time] .
	c. From the Meeting Start Time drop-down list, **select 9:00 AM.**
	Meeting start time: Tue 4/15/2003 ▼ 9:00 AM ▼
	d. **Click Propose Time.**
	e. In the message box, **type** *Can we meet in the morning instead?*
	f. **Click Send.**

TOPIC D

Track Meeting Responses

You have received meeting replies for various meetings you have scheduled. What do you do when you need to determine who will be attending those meetings? In this topic, you will track meeting responses.

You have a department meeting scheduled for tomorrow. You need to determine exactly how many people will be attending so that you can prepare the handouts. By using Outlook, you can quickly track who has responded and who has not responded to a meeting request.

How to Track Meeting Responses

Procedure Reference: Track Meeting Responses

To track meeting responses:

1. Display the Calendar.

2. Display the date on which the meeting is scheduled.

3. Double-click the meeting to open it.

4. Select the Tracking tab.

5. Click the Close button to close the Meeting form.

ACTIVITY 5-4

Tracking Meeting Responses

Setup:

The Inbox is displayed.

Scenario:

You've received several responses to the Vacation Policy meeting request you scheduled; however, you can't remember who accepted, declined, or hasn't responded. You need an accurate count so you will know how many handouts to make. In addition, you want to contact those who haven't responded.

What You Do	How You Do It
1. Display the meeting responses for the Vacation Policy meeting.	a. Display the Calendar.
	b. Display the date one week from the upcoming Tuesday.
	c. Double-click the Vacation Policy meeting that you scheduled to open its Meeting form.
	d. Select the Tracking tab.

2. True or False? You can determine that the meeting you opened is the one you sched-uled because the Attendance column indicates that you are the Meeting Organizer.

___ True

___ False

3. How can you determine who accepted and who declined the meeting invitation?

a) The Response column displays the replies.

b) A green check mark indicates an acceptance. A red X indicates a decline.

c) The user name displays in green when the user has accepted. The user name displays in red when the user has declined.

d) None of these.

4. Close the Meeting form.	a. Click the Close button.

TOPIC E

Update a Meeting Request

You have created a number of meeting requests. What if you discover that you need to change the location or time of one of those meetings? In this topic, you will update a meeting request.

You scheduled a meeting on the wrong day. You intended for the meeting to be on a Monday rather than a Tuesday. You could send cancellation notices and new meeting invites, but that will require a lot of work on your part and generate a lot of mail for all the attendees of the meeting. An easier and quicker solution is to reschedule the meeting by updating the meeting request.

How to Update a Meeting Request

Procedure Reference: Update a Meeting Request

To update a meeting request:

1. In the Calendar, open the Meeting form.

2. Make the appropriate changes to the Meeting form.

3. Send the update.

   a. If you want to notify attendees of the changes, on the Standard toolbar, click the Send Update To Attendees And Close button.

   b. If you don't need to notify the attendees of the changes, on the Standard toolbar, click Save And Close.

ACTIVITY 5-5

Updating a Meeting Request

Setup:

The date one week from the upcoming Tuesday is displayed in the Calendar.

Scenario:

You want to make sure that the attendees of the Vacation Policy meeting bring their concerns and suggestions with them to the meeting.

What You Do	How You Do It
1. For what reasons might you update a meeting request?	
2. Add a message to the Vacation Policy meeting you scheduled and send a meeting update.	a. Open the Vacation Policy Meeting form you scheduled.
	b. In the message body text box, **type** *Please bring your concerns and suggestions*.
	c. On the Standard toolbar, **click the Send Update To Attendees And Close button** Send Update .
3. Why might you choose to update a meeting request without sending an update?	

TOPIC F

Cancel a Meeting Request

You scheduled a meeting and edited meeting details. You also accepted meetings. Priorities change and emergencies happen so it's inevitable that schedules need to be adjusted. In this topic, you will cancel a meeting and notify attendees of the cancellation.

You have a meeting scheduled for tomorrow. A large number of participants are attending. You have a conflict, so you're going to have to cancel the meeting. You don't have time to call everyone. Luckily, you can use Outlook to quickly solve your problem. When you cancel a meeting in Outlook, each participant is automatically notified. Therefore, you won't have to worry about a participant showing up for a meeting that has been cancelled. In addition, participants' Calendars will be clear so they can attend other potential meetings instead.

How to Cancel a Meeting Request

Procedure Reference: Cancel a Meeting

To cancel a meeting:

1. In the Calendar, select the meeting entry that you want to cancel.

2. On the Standard toolbar, click Delete. A message box is displayed. The option to send a cancellation message and delete the meeting is selected.

    🖈 You can also delete a meeting without sending a cancellation message.

3. Click OK. A Meeting form is displayed.

4. If desired, in the Meeting form, enter a message.

5. Click Send to send the cancellation message.

ACTIVITY 5-6

Cancelling a Meeting Request

Setup:

The date one week from the upcoming Tuesday is displayed in the Calendar.

Scenario:

Something has come up, so you are not going to be able to go through with your staff's Vacation Policy meeting.

What You Do	How You Do It
1. **Cancel the Vacation Policy meeting you scheduled and send a cancellation message to all attendees.**	a. If necessary, in the Calendar, **select the Vacation Policy meeting that you scheduled.**
	b. On the Standard toolbar, **click Delete.**
	c. To send a cancellation message and delete the meeting, **click OK.**
	d. To send the cancellation message and remove the meeting from your Calendar, **click Send.**

TOPIC G

Print the Calendar

Now that you have created and modified several Calendar entries, your Calendar is up to date. What if you want to carry a hard copy of your appointments with you? In this topic, you will print the Calendar.

You are going to be out of the office on business. You have a number of meetings scheduled while you are away, but you won't have your computer with you. By printing a copy of your Calendar before you leave, you will know what your schedule is while you are away, and you won't have to worry about missing a meeting.

How to Print the Calendar

Procedure Reference: Print the Calendar

To print the Calendar:

1. With the Calendar open, on the Standard toolbar, click the Print button to display the Print dialog box.

2. From the Print Style list box, select a Calendar style.

3. In the Print Range box, specify the start date to designate the start time that you want printed.

4. In the Print Range box, specify the end date to designate the end time that you want printed.

5. If necessary, select other print options.

6. If desired, click Preview to display Print Preview.

7. If desired, click to zoom in.

8. If necessary, click Print to return to the Print dialog box.

9. Click OK to print the Calendar.

ACTIVITY 5-7

Printing the Calendar

Objective:
To preview and print the Calendar.

Setup:
The date one week from the upcoming Tuesday is displayed in the Calendar.

Scenario:
You're going to be out of the office for a few days attending a conference. You want to have your schedule with you while you are away if you need to refer to it.

What You Do	How You Do It
1. Set the print options to include the Monthly Style and to print the current month.	a. On the Standard toolbar, **click the Print button** .
	b. In the Print Style list box, **select Monthly Style.**
	c. In the Print Range box from the Start pop-up Calendar, **select the first day of the current month.**
	d. From the End pop-up Calendar, **select the last day of the current month.**
2. Preview the Calendar by zooming in and print the Calendar.	a. **Click Preview** to display the current month of your Calendar in Print Preview.
	b. **Click once** to zoom in.
	c. **Click Print** to close Print Preview and return to the Print dialog box.
	d. **Click OK** to print one copy of your Calendar.

Lesson 5 Follow-up

Great job! The task of organizing meetings has now been greatly simplified for you. You can use Outlook to organize meetings that involve any number of participants. You can use information available from their Calendars to schedule a meeting at a time that will work for all participants. You know how to keep track of who is coming to a meeting and who hasn't responded yet. When you receive a meeting request, you can send a reply to the meeting organizer. If you have to cancel a meeting, you know how to do it so that all participants are immediately notified of the cancellation.

1. **What were some things you had to take care of the last time you scheduled a meeting that would have been easier to do through the Calendar?**

2. **Have you ever tentatively agreed to a meeting? What were your reasons for tentatively accepting rather than accepting?**

LESSON 6
Managing Contacts

Lesson Time
40 minutes to 50 minutes

Lesson Objectives:

In this lesson, you will manage contacts and contact information.

You will:

*   Add a contact to the Outlook Address Book.

*   Sort contacts.

*   Find a contact.

*   Generate a map to a contact's location.

*   Edit a contact's information.

*   Delete a contact.

*   Print a list of contacts.

Introduction

You used the Inbox to send and receive messages, and you used the Calendar to schedule and cancel appointments and meetings—all with people within your organization. In this lesson, you will use the Contacts section to keep track of contacts outside of your organization.

You have quite a collection of business cards; however, that fax number you need in a hurry always seems hard to find. Outlook makes it easy to organize all the information you need about your business and personal associates. Names, addresses, and phone numbers are easily searchable and easy to retrieve and update.

TOPIC A

Add a Contact

Many of the tasks you've completed in Outlook have involved people within your organization. In the course of your workday, you have frequent interactions with people outside your organization, and they all have pieces of information, such as addresses, email addresses, work numbers, cell phone numbers, and fax numbers of which to keep track. In this topic, you will use the Contact section to help you keep track of all that information.

You send frequent mail messages to George Messerschmidt, a key client. Because he does not work for your company, his email address is not in the Global Address List. Every time you send him a message, you have to type his email address, which is georgemesserschmidt@msmoveandstore.com. Several times now you've misspelled the email address and the message bounced back to you as undeliverable. By adding George's email address to Outlook once, you can quickly retrieve it whenever you need it, saving typing time and avoiding misspellings and undeliverable messages.

Contacts

Definition:

A *contact* is a person with whom you communicate on a business or personal level and whose personal or business (or both) information is stored in the Contacts folder.

Example:

Figure 6-1 displays an example of a contact.

Abbott, Barbara C.	
Full Name:	Barbara C. Abbott
Home:	22 W. 188th St. Rochester, NY 14526
Business:	(585) 222-5555
Home:	(585) 222-2222
E-mail:	Babbott@teltronix.com
Categories:	Business

Figure 6-1: *An example of a contact.*

The Contact Form

When you create a new contact, Outlook displays a Contact form that contains tabs and text boxes in which you can enter personal and business information.

Figure 6-2 displays an example of a completed Contact form.

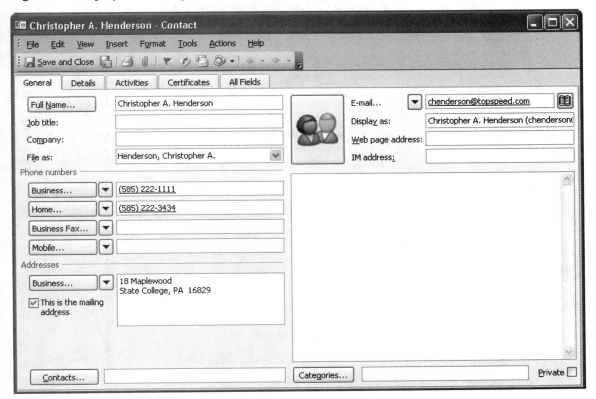

Figure 6-2: *A completed Contact form.*

The Outlook Address Book

Definition:

The *Outlook Address Book* is a list that contains all contacts that you create by using the Contact form.

Example:

Figure 6-3 displays the contents of an Outlook Address Book.

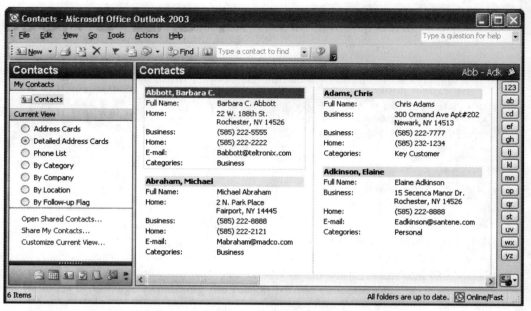

Figure 6-3: *The contents of an Outlook Address Book.*

How to Add a Contact

Procedure Reference: Add a Contact

To add a contact to the Outlook Address Book:

1. On the Go Menu, select Contacts to display the contents of the Contacts folder.

2. Display a new Contact form.
   - On the Standard toolbar, click the New Contact button.
   - Right-click and choose New Contact.
   - Choose File→New→Contact.
   - Choose Actions→New Contact.

3. Enter the desired information in the appropriate text boxes.

4. If desired, assign a contact to a category.
   a. Click Categories to display the Categories dialog box.
   b. In the Available Categories list box, check the appropriate category.
   c. Click OK.

5. On the Standard toolbar, click Save And Close.

ACTIVITY 6-1

Adding a Contact

Data Files:

- Andy Bloom.msg

Setup:

The Calendar is displayed.

Scenario:

Now that you're using email to communicate with people, you've obtained a lot of personal information. You would like to be able to store that information in one place, so that when you need to contact someone, you can quickly access that information.

You just met with a client who you will need to communicate with a lot via email and telephone. You want to store her contact information for future reference.

What You Do	How You Do It
1. With the Contacts folder displayed, display a new **Contact** form.	a. On the Go Menu, **select Contacts.**
	b. **Notice the Contacts in the Contacts folder.**
	c. On the Standard toolbar, **click the New Contact button** New ▾ . A new Contact form is displayed.
	d. **Maximize the Contact form.**
2. **Add Margaret Sherwood's name, title, which is Career Consultant, and company name, TekPro, to the form.**	a. In the Full Name text box, **type** *Margaret Sherwood*
	b. **Press Tab.**
	c. **Type** *Career Consultant*
	d. **Press Tab.**

e. In the Company text box, **type** *TekPro*

General	Details	Activities	Certifica

Full Name...   Margaret Sherwood

Job title: Career Consultant

Company: TekPro|

---

3. **Add Margaret's business and home phone numbers.**

a. In the Phone Numbers section in the Business text box, **type** *716-555-4444*

b. **Click in the Home text box.**

c. In the Location Information dialog box, in the first text box, **type** *585* **as the area code, and then click OK.**

d. In the dialog box, **click OK.**

e. In the Home text box, **type** *585-555-4445*

---

4. **Add Margaret's business and home address.**

a. **Click in the Addresses text box, and** type *Highland Parkway, Suite 301*

b. **Press Enter.**

c. **Type** *Buffalo, NY 14204*

Addresses

Business... ▼   Highland Parkway, Suite 301
Buffalo, NY 14204

d. From the Addresses drop-down list, **select Home.**

e. In the Addresses text box, **type** *222 Cullens Drive*

f. **Press Enter.**

g. **Type** *Rochester, NY 14622*

---

5. **Enter Margaret's email address.**

a. **Place the insertion point in the E-mail text box.**

b. **Type** *msherwood@tekpro.com*

---

6. **Assign this contact to the Business category.**

   a. At the bottom of the Contact form, click **Categories.**

   b. **Check Business.**

   c. **Click OK.**

7. **Take a few minutes to review the contents of the other tabs on the Contact form. What information can you document on the Contact form?**

   a) Pager number

   b) Mother's maiden name

   c) Phonetic name

   d) IM address

   e) Nickname

8. **Save and close the Contact form.**

TOPIC B

Sort Contacts

Your Outlook Address Book contains many contacts. What if you need to quickly display the contact information for all your business associates in a particular state? In this topic, you will sort contacts.

Outlook contains over 75 contacts for a particular client. You want to invite all of those contacts to an upcoming presentation. You printed your contact list, but it's in alphabetical order by name, so it's going to take time to locate all the employees for that one company. By sorting your contact list by company, you can quickly locate the names and addresses of all the contacts you want to invite to the presentation.

Sort Order

Definition:

Sort order is the sequence in which items are arranged.

Example:

Examples of different sort orders include:

- Ascending—A-Z
- Descending—Z-A

Figure 6-4 displays examples of contacts that are sorted in ascending and descending order.

Figure 6-4: *Examples of contacts sorted in descending and ascending order.*

How to Sort Contacts

Procedure Reference: Sort Contacts

To sort contacts:

1. Click any column header to sort by that header title. A small triangle to the right of the column name indicates that the list has been sorted by that column in a particular order.

2. Click the column header a second time to sort that column in reverse order.

 You can sort mail messages by using the View menu.

ACTIVITY 6-2

Sorting Contacts

Setup:
The Contacts folder is displayed.

Scenario:
You are sending invitations for an upcoming seminar at which you will be presenting. You want to send invitations to all your contacts at TekPro. Because the contacts are scattered throughout the list, you have to go through several pages of contact names to determine the ones you need. It would be much easier if you could display all TekPro contacts together on one page.

What You Do	How You Do It
1. **Display your Contacts as a phone list.**	a. In the Current View pane of the Navigation Pane, **select Phone List.**
2. **What happens when you place the mouse pointer over the Company header?** a) Nothing. b) The mouse pointer changes to a four-headed arrow. c) A ToolTip is displayed that says Sort by: Company. d) The header changes color.	
3. **Sort the list by company in alphabetical order.**	a. **Click the Company header.** 
4. **Sort the list by company name in reverse alphabetical order. Return the view to Address Cards.**	a. **Click the Company header again.** b. In the Current View pane, **select Address Cards.**

TOPIC C

Find a Contact

You added contacts and their information to the Contacts section. But having all that information is only useful if you can retrieve it quickly and efficiently. In this topic, you will find contact information.

You need to call a client. You know the name of his company, but you can't remember his name. By using Outlook's search feature, you can quickly locate the information for the client you need to contact by entering his company name.

How to Find a Contact

Procedure Reference: Find a Contact

To find a contact:

1. In the Find A Contact text box, click to activate the text box.

2. Type the name, company name, or other text on which you're going to search.

    🖈 If you have searched for this contact previously, you can click the Find A Contact drop-down arrow and select the contact name from the list.

3. Press Enter to display any contacts that match the word(s) you entered.

Searchable Terms

When you enter a word or phrase in the Find A Contact text box, Outlook looks in the Contact folder for a word or phrase that matches. By default, Outlook only searches for partial names, first or last names, email addresses, display as names, and company names.

ACTIVITY 6-3

Finding Contacts

Setup:
The Address Cards view of the Contacts folder is displayed.

Scenario:
You need to contact a client that you met with some time ago. You can't remember his full name, but when you met him last time he worked for Executive Recruiters.

What You Do	How You Do It
1. Search for the contact by using the company name.	a. Click in the Find A Contact text box.
	b. Type *Executive*
	Executive ▾
	c. Press Enter.

TOPIC D

Generate a Map

You added a number of contacts and you've seen how easy it is to find specific information about a contact. Now, you need to travel to a specific contact's location. In this topic, you will generate a map.

You have a meeting scheduled with a client at the client's location. You have the address, but you don't know how to get there. By using Outlook, you can quickly generate a map. You won't have to worry about being late for the meeting because you got lost.

How to Generate a Map

Procedure Reference: Generate a Map

To generate a map to a contact:

1. If necessary, display the Contact form of the contact for which you want to generate a map.

2. If necessary, from the Addresses drop-down list, select the address you want to map.

    🔖 You can generate a map to the address of any contact located in the United States.

3. On the Standard toolbar, click the Display Map Of Address button. A map to the contact's location is displayed in Internet Explorer.

4. If desired, click as needed to zoom in to the address on the map.

5. In the Internet Explorer window, click the Close button.

6. In the Contact form, click the Close button.

ACTIVITY 6-4

Generating a Map

Setup:

The Contact form for Andy Bloom is displayed.

Scenario:

You need to travel to one of your contact's locations. You only have his street address, and you're not sure how to get there.

What You Do	How You Do It
1. Display a map to Andy Bloom's business address and zoom in on the map.	a. On the Standard toolbar, **click the Display Map Of Address button** 🔲 . A map is displayed in Internet Explorer.
	b. If necessary, **maximize the Internet Explorer window.**
	c. **Click the address on the map twice** to zoom in to the address on the map.
2. Close Internet Explorer and the Contact form.	a. In the Internet Explorer window, **click the Close button.**
	b. In the Contact form, **click the Close button.**

TOPIC E

Edit a Contact

After you create and work with your contacts, you discover that some of the contact information has changed. In this topic, you will edit a contact.

Contact information changes frequently. Whether it's an updated address or phone number, you know what a hassle it is to cross out (or white out) information in your address book and squeeze in new information. Outlook puts an end to messy address books or card files. Your contact information will be neat and easy to read. You won't have to worry about dialing an incorrect phone number, because you misread a sloppy, handwritten number.

How to Edit a Contact

Procedure Reference: Edit a Contact

To edit a contact's information:

1. Open the Contact form that you want to edit.
    *   Double-click the Contact.
    *   Select the contact and choose File→Open→Selected Items.
    *   Right-click the contact and choose Open.
2. Edit the appropriate information.
3. Click Save And Close.

ACTIVITY 6-5

Editing a Contact

Setup:

The Address Cards view of the Contacts folder is displayed.

Scenario:

Melissa Lang, a job applicant who was just listed with your placement agency, was hired as a Programmer by Dynomite. Her email address is now lang@dynomite.com. Her manager's name is Beth Hilton. Your agency has a policy that all contact information must be kept up to date.

What You Do	How You Do It
1. Update Melissa's job title, company, and email address.	a. Double-click the address card for Melissa Lang to open her Contact form.
	b. Press Tab.
	c. Type *Programmer*
	d. In the Company text box, **type *Dynomite***
	e. In the E-mail text box, **type** *lang@dynomite.com*
2. Add the name of Melissa's manager and save the changes.	a. Select the Details tab.
	b. In the Manager's Name text box, **type** *Beth Hilton*
	c. Click Save And Close.

TOPIC F

Delete a Contact

You have some contact information that you no longer use. In this topic, you will delete a contact.

Your address book contains a number of contacts with whom you no longer do business. By deleting those old contacts, your address book will be less cluttered and you will save space on your hard drive.

How to Delete a Contact

Procedure Reference: Delete a Contact

There are a few different options for deleting a contact.

1. Delete a contact.

- Select the contact, and on the Standard toolbar, click the Delete button.
- Right-click the contact and choose Delete.
- Select the contact and choose Edit→Delete.

ACTIVITY 6-6

Deleting a Contact

Setup:
The Address Cards view of the Contacts folder is displayed.

Scenario:
One of your many applicants, for whom you have contact information, called you to inform you that she has moved out of state. She will no longer be needing the services of your agency.

What You Do	How You Do It
1. Delete the contact information for Gail Molina.	a. **Select the address card for Gail Molina.**
	b. On the Standard toolbar, **click the Delete button.**

TOPIC G

Print Contacts

Contact information is very useful when stored on your PC. However, what if you travel a lot and can't always access your contact information? In this topic, you will print contacts.

You will be out of the office on business. While you are away, you will be meeting with a number of contacts whose information is stored in your address book. You won't have your computer with you. By printing your contact list before you leave, you will have the appropriate information with you, so you can easily call or visit a contact.

How to Print Contacts

Procedure Reference: Print Contacts

To print contact information:

1. On the Standard toolbar, click the Print button to display the Print dialog box.

2. From the Print Style list box, select a print style.

3. If necessary, select other print options.

4. If desired, click Preview to display Print Preview.

5. If desired, click to zoom in.

6. If necessary, click Print to return to the Print dialog box.

7. Click OK to print the contacts.

Activity 6-7

Printing Contacts

Setup:
The Address Cards view of the Contacts folder is displayed.

Scenario:
You're going to be out of the office for a few days attending a conference. You want to meet with some of your contacts who are located in the same area as the conference. You'll need the addresses and telephone numbers of those contacts.

What You Do	How You Do It
1. **Display the Print dialog box.**	a. On the Standard toolbar, **click the Print button.**
2. **The default print style for Contacts is:** a) Card Style b) Small Booklet Style c) Medium Booklet Style d) Memo Style	
3. **Preview the contacts by zooming in and print the contacts.**	a. **Click Preview.** b. **Click on the contacts once** to zoom in. c. To close Print Preview and return to the Print dialog box, **click Print.** d. **Click OK.**

Lesson 6 Follow-up

Good work! You can now replace your messy rotary card file with a much more efficient system of storing information. You know how to create and maintain a contact list and how to access and view the list and individual contact information. You also know how to sort and find contacts and generate a map to a contact.

1. **What are some things that you frequently look up in your rotary card file that would be useful to store in the Outlook Contacts section?**

2. **What are some custom category names that you could create to help you organize your contacts?**

NOTES

LESSON 7
Managing Tasks

Lesson Objectives:

In this lesson, you will create and edit tasks.

You will:

- Create a task.
- Edit a task.
- Update a task.

Introduction

Communicating with messages, scheduling appointments and meetings, and organizing contact information are some common office procedures that you can accomplish with Outlook. You can also keep track of tasks by using Outlook. In this lesson, you will create and edit tasks, as well as mark them complete when they are done.

You are in the middle of writing a message and you think of something else that needs to be done. You could scribble yourself a note, hoping that it doesn't get lost in the shuffle. A better option is to enter the task in Outlook. Then, you will always have an electronic reminder of what needs to be done and when.

TOPIC A

Create a Task

Sometimes you might want to create a reminder for yourself about a project that doesn't need to go on your Calendar and you want to track its progress. In this topic, you will create a task.

When you schedule an appointment or meeting in Outlook, by default you are reminded about the appointment or meeting 15 minutes before the scheduled time. Similar to appointments and meetings, if you have tasks you need to accomplish, you can be reminded of those tasks by documenting them in Outlook. Then, you will have an electronic list of what you need to do and when you need to do it.

Task

Definition:

A *task* is an assigned piece of work that must be completed within a certain time frame.

Example:

Figure 7-1 displays some examples of tasks.

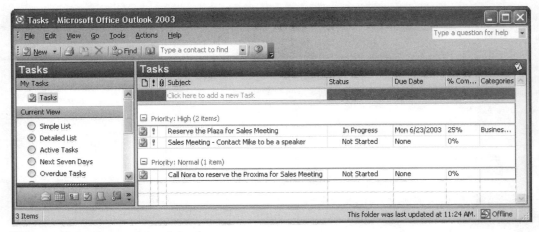

Figure 7-1: *Examples of tasks.*

The Task Form

The Task form contains the Task and Details tabs on which you can enter information for a task. Figure 7-2 displays an example of a completed Task Form.

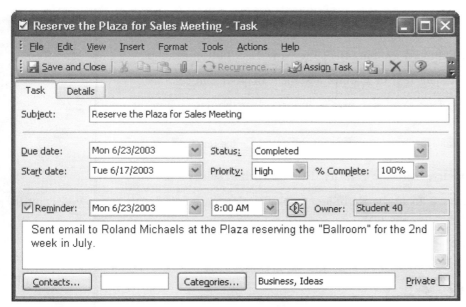

Figure 7-2: *An example of a completed Task Form.*

Task Form Options

Table 7-1 lists and describes some of the text boxes in the Task form.

Table 7-1: *Task Form Options*

Text Box	Description
Status	Displays one of five status choices: • Not Started • In Progress • Completed • Waiting On Someone Else • Deferred
Priority	Low, Normal, High.
% Complete	How far along on the task you are.
Note area	Any additional notes about the task.
Categories	You can assign a category to a task.
Total Work	Used for entering the estimated hours.
Actual Hours	Used for entering the actual hours.
Companies	Used for entering companies which you need to bill for services.

How to Create a Task

Procedure Reference: Create a Task

To create a task:

1. If necessary, display the Tasks list.

2. On the Standard toolbar, click the New Task button to display a new Task form.

3. In the Subject text box, enter a subject of your choice.

4. From the Due Date pop-up Calendar, select the date when the task is due.

   ✒ You can type Today, Tomorrow, or enter a date in the Due Date text box.

5. If necessary, from the Priority drop-down list, select a priority.

6. If necessary, from the Reminder pop-up Calendar, select a date when you want to be reminded of the task.

7. On the Standard toolbar, click Save And Close.

ACTIVITY 7-1

Creating a Task

Setup:
The Contacts folder is displayed.

Scenario:
You need to determine the system requirements within one week for a high-priority inventory meeting. You would like to be reminded about the meeting the day before you meet.

It's also a high priority that you meet with Mike regarding the system requirements for the inventory. A lunch meeting needs to be scheduled today.

What You Do	How You Do It
1. **Display the Task list and view the column header names.**	a. On the Go Menu, **click Tasks.** The Tasks list is displayed.
	b. Using ToolTips, **view the column header names.**
2. **In the Tasks list, the second column from the left is the _____ column.**	
a) Icon	
b) Subject	
c) Due Date	
d) Complete	

3. **Display a new Task form and enter a subject of *Determine system requirements for inventory*. Enter the date one week from today.**

a. On the Standard toolbar, **click the New Task button** 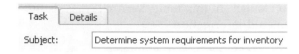 to display a new Task form.

b. In the Subject text box, **type *Determine system requirements for inventory***

c. **Click the Due Date drop-down arrow.**

d. **Select the date one week from today.** The selected date is displayed in the Due Date text box.

4. **Set the priority to High. Set a reminder for six days from today. Save and close the Task form.**

a. From the Priority drop-down list, **select High.**

Priority: High

b. From the Reminder pop-up Calendar, **select the date six days from today.**

c. On the Standard toolbar, **click Save And Close.**

5. **Create a task for scheduling lunch with Mike. The task needs to be completed today, so it's a high priority.**

a. **Display a new Task form.**

b. **Enter a subject of *Schedule lunch with Mike***

c. **Set the due date to today.**

d. **Set the priority to High.**

e. **Save and close the Task form.**

TOPIC B

Edit a Task

You have entered information for an upcoming task. But like everything else, tasks are liable to change. In this topic, you will make some changes to the task by updating previously entered information.

You created a task to complete the monthly slide show presentation by Friday. Your manager tells you it needs to be completed a day earlier. You could create a new task, but it would be easier to edit the existing task. You can quickly edit the date of the task, ensuring that the task information is accurate.

How to Edit a Task

Procedure Reference: Edit a Task

To edit a task:

1. If necessary, display the Tasks list.

2. Open the task you want to edit.

3. Make the appropriate changes to the Task form.

4. Save and close the Task form.

ACTIVITY 7-2

Editing a Task

Setup:

The Tasks list is displayed.

Scenario:

You just discovered that Mike isn't the person who is going to be handling the system requirements for the inventory. It's Joe instead. Therefore, you need to go to lunch with Joe instead of Mike. Also, the due date for the system requirements for the inventory has changed to the upcoming Thursday.

What You Do	How You Do It
1. Edit the Schedule lunch with Mike task so that it states *Schedule lunch with Joe*.	a. Double-click the Schedule lunch with Mike task to open the Task form. 🖈 You can also select the item you want to edit and press Enter to open it. b. In the Subject text box, **double-click the word Mike** to select it. c. Type *Joe* Subject: Lunch with Joe d. Save and close the Task form.
2. Change the date of the Determine system requirements for inventory task to the upcoming Thursday.	a. Open the Determine system requirements for inventory Task form. b. Change the due date to the upcoming Thursday. c. Save and close the Task form.

TOPIC C

Update a Task

You have entered a task and edited information about the task. What do you do with a task item when you are finished? In this topic, you will indicate that a task has been completed.

You have completed the monthly slide show presentation. You want to indicate that on the task list. By updating the status of the task, it will display as complete, making it easy for you to quickly track the progress of that task or any other task on the list.

How to Update a Task

Procedure Reference: Update a Task

To update a task:

1. If necessary, display the Tasks list.

2. In the Complete column, check the check box of the task you have completed. The task is marked as completed and is crossed off.

ACTIVITY 7-3

Updating a Task

Setup:
The Tasks list is displayed.

Scenario:
You just scheduled lunch with Joe to discuss the system requirements for the inventory. Therefore, you have completed that task.

What You Do	How You Do It
1. Mark the Schedule lunch with Joe task as complete.	a. In the Complete column for the Schedule lunch with Joe task, **check the check box** to mark the task complete.

2. How does the display of the Schedule lunch with Joe task change?

    a) The task is moved to the end of the Tasks list.

    b) The task is displayed with a check mark and is moved to the end of the Tasks list.

    c) The task is displayed with a check mark and is crossed off.

    d) The task is displayed with a check mark only.

Lesson 7 Follow-up

Well done! Getting organized is critical to accomplishing tasks efficiently. You now know how to create tasks so that you know, at a glance, everything you have to accomplish. You also know how to edit tasks so that they are always up-to-date, as well as how to update a task once you're done.

1. How could a task list help you accomplish your job more efficiently?

2. When you are working on a project, what kinds of information do you have to keep track of that could be stored in the task list?

LESSON **8**
Using Notes

Lesson Time
20 minutes to 30 minutes

Lesson Objectives:

In this lesson, you will create and edit notes.

You will:

- Create a note.
- Edit a note.
- Move a note.

Introduction

So far, you've seen how a number of Outlook components can help you work more efficiently. Another common task you probably do regularly is make notes to yourself, so that you don't forget something. Wouldn't it be nice if you could do this electronically? In this lesson, you will create, edit, and move notes.

You have paper notes with writing scattered all over your desk. What if you misplace or accidentally throw away one of those notes? Instead, you can use Outlook to electronically store your thoughts and ideas as notes and easily reference or update those notes whenever needed.

TOPIC A

Create a Note

In Outlook, you have a place for everything. You can communicate by using the Inbox and schedule appointments and meetings in the Calendar. You can store information about business and personal contacts and keep track of tasks. What if you need to jot down an idea or thought? In this topic, you will use notes to do that.

While composing a message, you think of an issue you want bring up at the next department meeting. You could stop what you're doing and work on the meeting item, but you really want to complete the message first. By using Outlook, you can quickly document your thoughts and ideas for easy reference later. You won't have to worry about misplacing your thoughts and ideas that you scribbled on a piece of paper.

How to Create a Note

Procedure Reference: Create a Note

To create a note:

1. In the Navigation Pane on the Quick Launch bar, click the Notes button to display the Notes folder.

2. On the Standard toolbar, click the New Note button to display a new note.

3. Enter the contents of the note.

4. If necessary, assign the note to a category.

    a. Click the Note icon and choose Categories to display the Categories dialog box.

    b. From the Available Categories list box, check the category to which you want to assign the note.

    c. Click OK.

5. If necessary, place the mouse pointer on the resizing handle until a double-headed arrow is displayed and drag to resize the note.

6. Click the Close button to close the note.

ACTIVITY 8-1

Creating a Note

Objective:

To create a note, assign it to a category, and resize the note.

Setup:

The Tasks list is displayed.

Scenario:

You're in the middle of working on a project, when you remember that you want to clarify for your employees the company policy regarding personal email. You will add it to the meeting agenda later, but for now you just want to jot it down somewhere so you don't forget it.

What You Do	How You Do It
1. In the Notes folder, **display a new Note.**	a. In the Navigation Pane on the Quick Launch bar, **click the Notes button** [icon] .
	b. On the Standard toolbar, **click the New Note button** [New] to display a new Note.

2. **What is displayed at the bottom of a note?**

   a) The system date and time.

   b) The date and time the note was created.

   c) Only the date the note was created.

   d) The system date.

   e) Only the time the note was created.

3. **Write a note to remind yourself about this item and assign it to the Business category.**	a. Type *Meeting Reminder: company policy regarding personal email.*
	b. In the upper-left corner of the note, **click the Note icon and choose Categories.**
	c. **Check Business.**
	d. **Click OK.**

4. **Decrease the size of the note and close it.**

a. **Place the mouse pointer on the resizing handle until a double-headed arrow is displayed.**

Click and drag up and to the left to resize the note.

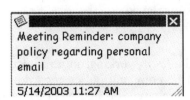

b. **Click the Close button.**

5. **Change the view of the Notes folder to Categories, and return the view to Icons.**

a. **In the Navigation Pane, select By Category.**

b. **Click Icons** to return the view to the default.

TOPIC B

Edit a Note

After you create a note, you might want to add or delete information from that note. In this topic, you will edit the contents of a note.

You created a note for an issue that you want to discuss at the next department meeting. You have been thinking about the issue, and you want to jot down additional thoughts and ideas. By editing an existing note, you ensure that your thoughts and ideas are accurately documented and related information will be stored in the same place.

How to Edit a Note

Procedure Reference: Edit a Note

To edit a note:

1. If necessary, display the Notes folder.

2. Open the note you want to edit by using one of the following methods:
    *   If the note is selected, press Enter.
    *   Double-click the note.
    *   Right-click the note and choose Open.

3. Edit the contents of the note as desired.

4. If necessary, resize the note.

5. Close the note.

ACTIVITY 8-2

Editing a Note

Setup:

The Notes folder is displayed.

Scenario:

You just remembered that in addition to clarifying the company's policy on personal email, you want to make sure you distribute a copy of the company policy to the employees.

What You Do	How You Do It
1. Edit the contents of the note so that the words "present and distribute" are displayed before the word "company."	a. With the note selected, **press Enter** to open it.
	b. **Place the insertion point before the word "company."**
	Meeting Reminder: company policy regarding personal email
	c. Type *present and distribute*
	d. **Press Spacebar.**
	e. If necessary, **resize the note.**
	f. **Close the note.**

TOPIC C

Copy a Note

You created a note and edited it. To be more organized, you want the note to display in a different location. In this topic, you will copy a note.

You have captured a number of ideas relating to an issue you want to discuss at the next department meeting. You don't want to forget to mention the issue at the scheduled time. By copying the note to your desktop, the issue will be visible as soon as you log in the morning of the meeting, reminding you that you want to discuss the issue.

How to Copy a Note

Procedure Reference: Copy a Note

To copy a note to the desktop:

1. If necessary, display the Notes folder.

2. Adjust the size of the Outlook window so that the desktop is visible.

3. Drag the note you want to copy to the desktop.

📌 You can also copy or move a note to a folder.

ACTIVITY 8-3

Copying a Note

Setup:
The Notes folder is displayed.

Scenario:
You created a note for yourself to add an item to a meeting agenda. You know that if you leave the note in the Notes folder, you might forget about it once you open another application. If the Note was on your desktop, it would be much more visible.

What You Do	How You Do It
1. Adjust the size of the Outlook window so that the desktop is visible.	a. Click the Restore Down button .
	b. If necessary, so that the contents of the Notes folder and the desktop are visible, position the mouse pointer over any corner of the window and adjust the size of the window.

2. Copy the note to your desktop. Maximize the Outlook window.

   a. **Drag the note from the Notes folder to the desktop.** A copy of the note is displayed on the desktop.

   b. **Click the Maximize button.**

Lesson 8 Follow-up

The Outlook Notes section allows you to capture those miscellaneous bits of information that you don't want to lose or forget. You know how to enter information into a note, edit a note, and move a note.

1. **What are some things that you frequently jot down on sticky notes that would be suitable for Outlook notes?**

2. **How do you think using notes could be helpful to you in your job?**

Follow-up

Congratulations! You've mastered the critical skills that you need to begin communicating by using Outlook 2003.

1. **Of the tools covered in this course, which one(s) will you use the most? Which one(s) will you use the least?**

2. **What do you feel is the biggest advantage of using Outlook 2003? Why? What is the biggest disadvantage of using Outlook 2003? Why?**

What's Next?

This course is the first in a series. After completing this course, students might be interested in expanding their knowledge of Microsoft® Outlook® 2003 by taking *Microsoft Outlook 2003: Level 2* and *Microsoft Outlook 2003: Level 3*.

APPENDIX A

Microsoft Office Specialist Program

Selected Element K courseware addresses Microsoft Office Specialist skills. The following tables indicate where Outlook® 2003 skills are covered. For example, 1-3 indicates the lesson and activity number applicable to that skill.

Core Skill Sets and Skills Being Measured	Outlook® 2003: Level 1	Outlook® 2003: Level 2	Outlook® 2003: Level 3
Originate and Respond to E-mail and Instant Messages			
Addressing e-mail messages and instant messages to recipients	1-3, 2-1		1-3
Forwarding and replying to e-mail messages and instant messages	1-5, 2-5		1-3
Attach Files to Items			
Inserting attachments to e-mail and instant messages	2-4		1-4
Create and Modify a Personal Signature for Message			
Creating and modifying e-mail signatures			2-3, 2-4, 2-5
Creating unique e-mail signatures for multiple accounts			2-3, 2-4
Modify E-mail Message Settings and Delivery Options			
Flagging e-mail messages	3-2		
Formatting e-mail messages (e.g., HTML, Rich Text, and Plain Text)		3-3	
Setting e-mail message importance and sensitivity		3-1	
Setting e-mail message delivery options		3-2	

Core Skill Sets and Skills Being Measured	Outlook® 2003: Level 1	Outlook® 2003: Level 2	Outlook® 2003: Level 3
Create and Edit Contacts			
Adding contacts and contact information to e-mail and Instant Messenger	6-1		1-2
Updating and modifying contact information	6-5		
Accept, Decline, and Delegate Tasks			
Accepting, declining, and delegating tasks		5-1, 5-2	
Create, Modify Appointments, Meetings, and Events			
Adding appointments to the calendar	4-2		
Scheduling meetings and inviting attendees	5-1		
Scheduling resources for meetings	5-1		
Scheduling events	4-4		
Update, Cancel, and Respond to Meeting Requests			
Accepting and declining meeting requests	5-2		
Proposing new meeting times	5-3		
Updating and cancelling meeting requests	5-5, 5-6		
Customize Calendar Settings			
Setting calendar options		2-2, 2-3	
Setting work days and times		2-1	
Create, Modify, and Assign Tasks			
Creating, modifying, and assigning tasks	7-1, 7-2, 7-3	5-1	
Create and Modify Distribution Lists			
Creating and modifying distribution lists		3-5, 3-6	
Link Contacts to Other Items			
Tracking activities for contacts			4-5
Create and Modify Notes			
Creating and editing notes	8-1, 8-2		
Organize Items			
Adding and deleting fields			6-1
Sorting items	6-2	7-1	
Filtering messages		7-4	
Organizing items using colors, rules, and views	4-5, 6-2	7-5, 7-6, 7-7	3-3, 3-4
Organize Items Using Folders			

Core Skill Sets and Skills Being Measured	Outlook® 2003: Level 1	Outlook® 2003: Level 2	Outlook® 2003: Level 3
Creating and deleting folders for items	3-3, 3-6		
Moving items between folders	3-4, 3-5		
Archiving items			5-2
Search for Items			
Finding items	6-3	7-2, 7-3	
Using Search folders			3-2
Save Items in Different File Formats			
Saving items in different file formats (e.g., .htm or .txt)			5-1
Assign Items to Categories			
Assigning items to categories	6-1, 8-1		
Preview and Print Items			
Previewing and printing items	1-6, 5-7, 6-7		

NOTES

LESSON LABS

Due to classroom setup constraints, some labs cannot be keyed in sequence immediately following their associated lesson. Your instructor will tell you whether your labs can be practiced immediately following the lesson or whether they require separate setup from the main lesson content.

LESSON 1 LAB 1

Creating and Replying to a Message

Scenario:

Your company hired a new employee who works in a different location. Eventually, you will be working with her. You don't know anything about her, but you would like to get to know her.

1. **Create and send a message describing yourself to your partner.** You can include anything you want in your message, or you can use the following suggestions:
   - Your name, the name of your company, your primary responsibilities, and your reason(s) for attending class.
   - Your name and what you like to do in your spare time.

2. When you receive the message from your partner, **send a reply.**

3. If necessary, **close the original message.**

4. **Open and read the reply.**

5. **Close the reply.**

LESSON 2 LAB 1

Creating a Message Using the Global Address List and Forwarding a Message

Scenario:

You have a friend who is interested in working at TekPro. She has given you her resume, and she'd like you to pass it on to your manager. She does not have access to email.

Your manager is very impressed with your friend's resume. He wants his manager to take a look at it also.

1. **Create a new message, and address the message to your partner by using the Global Address List.**

2. **Add appropriate subject and message text of your choice.**

3. **Apply the formatting of your choice to the message text.**

4. **Attach the file SS Resume to the message.**

5. **Check the message for spelling and grammar errors.**

6. **Send the message to your partner.**

7. **Forward the message received from your partner to someone else in the class.**

LESSON 3 LAB 1

Managing Mail

Scenario:

As the job fair coordinator, you know that staying organized is key to your success. You have a number of messages in your Inbox that relate to an upcoming job fair. It would be easier to refer to those messages if they were together in one location.

1. In the Inbox folder, **create a subfolder called** *Job Fair*

2. **Move a message of your choice into the new folder.**

LESSON 4 LAB 1

Using the Calendar

Scenario:

You are coaching your company's soccer team this season. The practices are at Hyde Park, from 4:30 PM to 7:30 PM every Thursday through the next two months.

1. **Open a new Appointment form and set a recurring appointment with the subject of** *Soccer* **and a location of** *Hyde Park* **for every Thursday from 4:30 PM to 7:30 PM through the next two months.**

2. **Save and close the Appointment form.**

3. **Check your Calendar to verify that the repeating appointment has been scheduled.**

LESSON 5 LAB 1

Scheduling Meetings

Setup:

Your assigned partner is also performing this practice activity and you have decided who is User A and who is User B.

Scenario:

You need to meet with a colleague to discuss budget requirements for next year. You've checked his Calendar and discovered that you are both available this coming Thursday (User A at 10:30 AM and User B at 2:30 PM).

Just when you receive an acceptance to your scheduled budget meeting, you are asked by your manager to travel out of town that day. So, you cancel the meeting, sending a cancellation notice that includes a message explaining the reason for the cancellation.

User A:

1. Schedule a one-hour *Budget* meeting with your partner for this coming Thursday at 10:30 AM.

User B:

2. Schedule a one-hour *Budget* meeting with your partner for this coming Thursday at 2:30 PM.

Users A and B:

3. Accept the meeting request, including a message of your choice.

Users A and B:

4. Cancel the Budget meeting you scheduled, sending a cancellation notice that includes a message explaining why it's being cancelled.

LESSON 6 LAB 1

Creating Contacts

Scenario:

You met a placement specialist at a recent training conference you attended. You don't want to lose his contact information, which is listed below:

Name: Roger Gorman

Business address: 23 Colonial Way, Syracuse, NY 14388

Business phone: 315–555–9090

E-mail address: rogergorman@anytown.com

Home address: 33 Sylvia Way, Baldwinsville, NY 14378

After reviewing your contacts in various views, you remember to include "Rog" as a nick-name for the newly added contact.

---

1. Using the scenario, **add the contact to the Outlook Address Book.**

---

2. **Save and close the Contact form.**

---

3. **View your contacts in different views.**

---

4. **Include *Rog* as a nickname for the newly added contact.**

---

5. **Save and close the Contact form.**

LESSON 7 LAB 1

Using the Task List

Scenario:

You are in charge of an upcoming job fair at a local community college. Among the many tasks that you must complete is a telephone meeting with the college coordinator this coming Tuesday to discuss your space requirements. A reminder the afternoon before the meeting would be great. Later you realize that you need to discuss more than just space requirements. You also need to discuss job fair requirements.

1. **Create a task for the telephone call with the appropriate due date and reminder.**

2. **Edit the task subject to state** *Job Fair Requirements*.

LESSON 8 LAB 1

Creating Notes

Scenario:

You're in the middle of a conference call regarding some new company policies. While you're listening, many thoughts are running through your head. You want to document those thoughts so you can refer to them after the call.

1. **In the Notes folder, create two notes with the contents of your choice.**

2. **Assign each of the notes to an appropriate category.**

3. **Close the notes.**

SOLUTIONS

Lesson 1

Activity 1-1

3. **What components of the Outlook window look familiar to you?**

   Answers will vary, but might include: The title bar, the menu bar, the window control buttons, and the status bar.

Activity 1-2

1. **Match the components of the Outlook window with their corresponding definitions.**

_c_	Navigation Pane	a.	Displays the contents of the selected message without opening the message.
_e_	Quick Launch bar	b.	Displays information about the active folder.
_d_	Go Menu	c.	The column on the left side of the Outlook window that provides access to all components of Outlook.
_a_	Reading Pane	d.	Part of the Navigation Pane that allows you to quickly switch between Mail, Calendar, Contacts, and Tasks.
_b_	Status bar	e.	Part of the Navigation Pane that provides quick access through buttons to frequently used Outlook components.

Activity 1-4

1. **How does a new, unread message display in the Inbox?**

   ✓ a) The header is bold.

      b) The header is red.

   ✓ c) The header contains a closed envelope symbol.

      d) The header contains an open envelope symbol.

   ✓ e) The header contains the sender's user name.

Activity 1-5

2. **When you create a reply to a message, the color of the reply text is** _blue_ .

4. After you send a reply, what is displayed in the InfoBar of the original message?

    a) Only the date you replied.

    b) Only the time you replied.

    ✓ c) The date and time you replied.

    d) The message "Your reply was sent."

6. How does a message that you have replied to display in the Inbox?

    a) The header is bold.

    b) The header only contains an open envelope symbol.

    ✓ c) The header is not bold.

    ✓ d) The header contains an open envelope symbol with an arrow pointing left.

    e) The header contains an open envelope symbol with an arrow pointing right.

Activity 1-6

2. The default number of copies is set to _1_ .

3. The default page range is set to _All_ .

Activity 1-7

3. True or False? The New Job Posting message is displayed in the Deleted Items folder.

    ✓ True

    __ False

Activity 2-2

2. The default font style of the message text is:

    a) Arial 12

    ✓ b) Arial 10

    c) Times New Roman 10

    d) Times New Roman 12

Activity 2-3

1. True or False? The wavy red underline below the word Teknology indicates that there is a possible spelling error with the word.

    ✓ True

    __ False

3. True or False? After you correct any spelling errors, the word Teknology displays with the wavy red underline.

    __ True

    ✓ False

Activity 2-4

1. **What types of files will you attach to your messages?**

   Answers will vary, but might include: Meeting agendas, spreadsheets, presentations, and graphics.

3. **In the Inbox, how can you tell that a message contains an attachment?**

   a) The header contains the word Attachment.

   b) The header contains the word Attachment and an attachment symbol.

   ✓ c) An attachment symbol is displayed to the right of the subject text.

   d) The header doesn't contain any information to indicate that a message contains an attachment.

Activity 2-5

2. **What text boxes in a forwarded Message form are prepopulated with text?**

   a) To

   b) Cc

   ✓ c) Subject

   ✓ d) Attach

   ✓ e) Message body

3. **In addition to the Subject text, what is displayed in the Subject text box of a message that indicates that the message will be or has been forwarded?**

   ✓ a) FW:

   b) Forward:

   c) Frwd:

   d) Forwarded:

Lesson 3

Activity 3-1

2. **True or False? The contents of the attachment include a resume for Samantha J. Alvarez.**

   ✓ True

   ___ False

SOLUTIONS

Activity 3-2

2. **After you flag a message for follow-up, how does it display in the Inbox?**

    a) A red flag symbol is displayed to the left of the header.

    b) A green flag symbol is displayed to the right of the header.

    c) A green flag symbol is displayed to the left of the header.

    d) A blue flag symbol is displayed to the right of the header.

    ✓ e) A red flag symbol is displayed to the right of the header.

4. **True or False? The Multimedia Developer message you flagged for follow-up is displayed in the For Follow Up folder.**

    ✓ True

    ___ False

Activity 3-3

2. **True or False? In the All Mail Folders pane of the Navigation Pane, the Resumes folder is displayed below the Inbox.**

    ✓ True

    ___ False

Activity 3-5

2. **What information does the System Training message contain?**

    a) Information on system training only.

    b) Information on system training and vacation.

    ✓ c) Information on system training and health insurance.

    d) Information on system training and retirement plans.

Activity 3-6

2. **True or False? In the All Mail Folders pane, the Deleted Items folder indicates that it contains items.**

    ✓ True

    ___ False

Lesson 4

Activity 4-1

2. **Match the types of Calendar entries with their corresponding definitions.**

    <u>c</u>   Appointment

    <u>b</u>   Event

    <u>a</u>   Meeting

    a. Appointment that involves scheduling with other participants and resources.

    b. Activity that is associated with a specific day (or group of days) and a year, but not with a specific time.

    c. Reservation of a time slot for a designated purpose.

Activity 4-2

4. **The default reminder for an appointment is:**

    a) 5 minutes

    b) 10 minutes

    ✓ c) 15 minutes

    d) 20 minutes

6. **What does the symbol that is displayed with the new appointment indicate?**

    a) The appointment is recurring.

    ✓ b) The appointment has a reminder.

    c) The appointment is private.

Activity 4-3

3. **How is the Appointment form different after you set the recurrence options?**

    ✓ a) The InfoBar indicates the day of the week, the dates the meeting will occur, and at what time.

    ✓ b) The title bar indicates that the appointment is now recurring.

    ✓ c) The Starting Time and Ending Time fields are no longer displayed.

    d) The reminder is now set to 30 minutes.

    e) The InfoBar indicates the dates of the meetings only.

5. **What do the symbols that are displayed with the appointment indicate?**

    a) The appointment has a reminder only.

    b) The appointment is private.

    c) The appointment is recurring only.

    ✓ d) The appointment has a reminder and is recurring.

Activity 4-4

4. **True or False? Events do not occupy blocks of time in your Calendar.**

   ✓ True

   ___ False

5. **Events appear in _banners_ at the top of the date(s) you specified in the Calendar.**

6. **In addition to the banner at the top of the Appointment Section, how is the training event represented in your Calendar?**

   ✓ a) A purple banner is displayed on the specified dates.

   b) A white banner is displayed on the specified dates.

   c) A blue banner is displayed on the specified dates.

   d) A green banner is displayed on the specified dates.

Activity 4-6

1. **Why might you need to update a Calendar entry?**

   Answers will vary, but might include: The date, time, or location of an appointment changes.

3. **When you entered a new start time, what happened to the end time?**

   a) It stayed the same.

   b) It automatically changed to 2:00 PM.

   ✓ c) It automatically changed to 2:30 PM.

   d) None of these.

Lesson 5

Activity 5-1

5. **Are Conference Room A and the TV VCR listed with the other meeting attendees?**

   Yes

Activity 5-4

2. **True or False? You can determine that the meeting you opened is the one you scheduled because the Attendance column indicates that you are the Meeting Organizer.**

   ✓ True

   ___ False

3. **How can you determine who accepted and who declined the meeting invitation?**

   ✓ a) The Response column displays the replies.

   b) A green check mark indicates an acceptance. A red X indicates a decline.

   c) The user name displays in green when the user has accepted. The user name displays in red when the user has declined.

   d) None of these.

Activity 5-5

1. **For what reasons might you update a meeting request?**

   Answers will vary, but might include: To change the subject, location, date, time, or message.

3. **Why might you choose to update a meeting request without sending an update?**

   Answers will vary, but might include: The information you're updating doesn't affect the attendees (for example, you changed the length of the reminder time).

Lesson 6

Activity 6-1

7. **Take a few minutes to review the contents of the other tabs on the Contact form. What information can you document on the Contact form?**

   ✓ a) Pager number

   b) Mother's maiden name

   c) Phonetic name

   ✓ d) IM address

   ✓ e) Nickname

Activity 6-2

2. **What happens when you place the mouse pointer over the Company header?**

   a) Nothing.

   b) The mouse pointer changes to a four-headed arrow.

   ✓ c) A ToolTip is displayed that says Sort by: Company.

   d) The header changes color.

Activity 6-7

2. **The default print style for Contacts is:**

    ✓ a) Card Style

    b) Small Booklet Style

    c) Medium Booklet Style

    d) Memo Style

Lesson 7

Activity 7-1

2. **In the Tasks list, the second column from the left is the _____ column.**

    a) Icon

    b) Subject

    c) Due Date

    ✓ d) Complete

Activity 7-3

2. **How does the display of the Schedule lunch with Joe task change?**

    a) The task is moved to the end of the Tasks list.

    b) The task is displayed with a check mark and is moved to the end of the Tasks list.

    ✓ c) The task is displayed with a check mark and is crossed off.

    d) The task is displayed with a check mark only.

Lesson 8

Activity 8-1

2. **What is displayed at the bottom of a note?**

    a) The system date and time.

    ✓ b) The date and time the note was created.

    c) Only the date the note was created.

    d) The system date.

    e) Only the time the note was created.

GLOSSARY

Address Book
A collection of address books or address lists that you can use to find and select names, email addresses, and distribution lists to quickly address messages.

Appointment Section
A section of the Calendar that displays your schedule for one day in specified time slots.

attachment
A copy of any type of file or an Outlook item that you can add to an Outlook item and then separate from the Outlook item.

category
A keyword or phrase that you can assign to related items so that you can easily track the items.

contact
A person with whom you communicate on a business or personal level and whose information is stored in the Contacts folder.

Date Navigator
A section of the Calendar, displayed as two adjacent months, that you can use to navigate in the Calendar.

email
An application that allows a user to create, send, and receive electronic messages.

email address
A string used to specify the user name and the location where users can send you email.

folder
A tool that you can use to store and organize Outlook items.

Global Address List
A list of all user names and global distribution lists in a particular organization that is created and maintained by the Microsoft Exchange Server Administrator.

InfoBar
Displays information about what has occurred or what action you need to take, and is displayed below the active toolbar.

item
A basic element created in Outlook that holds information and is stored in a specific location.

meeting resource
An item with its own email account on the Microsoft Exchange Server that you can schedule for a meeting, and it will automatically accept or reject meeting invitations.

Net etiquette (Network etiquette)
Proper guidelines users should follow when communicating electronically across a network.

Outlook Address Book
A list that contains all contacts that you create by using the Contact form.

sort order
The sequence in which items are arranged.

spamming
The act of sending unsolicited advertisements to email recipients or newsgroups.

task
An assigned piece of work that you do regularly or just once that must be completed within a certain time frame.

GLOSSARY

view
A way to display items in an Outlook folder.

INDEX

A

Address Book, 26

Appointment forms, 55

appointments

assigning a category to, 64

deleting, 68

editing, 68

recurring, 59

reminders, 57

scheduling, 57

attachments, 33

opening, 40

saving, 40

AutoCorrect, 30

C

Calendar

Appointment Section, 53

Date Navigator, 53

entries, 52

printing, 88

symbols, 56

views, 53

category, 64

Contact form, 93

contacts, 92

adding, 94

deleting, 104

editing, 103

finding, 100

printing, 105

sorting, 98

E

email, 10

email address, 12

emoticons, 13

Also See: smileys

events

creating, 61

F

files

attaching, 34

size, 33

type, 33

flaming, 14

folders, 7

creating, 44

deleting, 49

G

Global Address List, 27

grammar checking, 31

H

Help, 9

I

InfoBar, 18

item, 6

M

maps

generating, 101

Meeting form, 73

meeting requests

accepting, 78

declining, 78

meeting resource, 74

meetings

canceling, 86

conflicts, 79

online, 76

proposing a new time, 81

scheduling, 72

tracking responses, 83

updating requests, 85

Message forms, 11

INDEX

messages
  addressing, 27
  composing, 12
  copying to a folder, 48
  deleting, 22
  flagging, 42
  formatting, 29
  forwarding, 35
  marking unread, 43
  moving to folders, 46
  opening, 16
  printing, 20
  recalling, 31
  recovering deleted, 22
  replying to, 18
  saving, 14
  sending, 12
  symbols, 16

N
net etiquette, 13
notes
  copying, 123
  creating, 118
  editing, 121

O
Outlook
  components, 5
  logging on to, 3
Outlook Address Book, 93

S
smileys, 13
    Also See: emoticons
sort order, 97
spamming, 14
spell checking, 31

T
Task form, 111
tasks, 110
  creating, 112
  editing, 114
  updating, 115

V
views, 52